JULY 4/06

THE COMPANY YOU KEEP

STEVE

THANKS FOR
YOUR KINDNESS TODAY!

ENJOY,

David

THE

THE TRANSFORMING POWER

COMPANY

OF MALE FRIENDSHIP

YOU KEEP

DAVID C. BENTALL

MINNEAPOLIS

Cover design by David Meyer
Cover photo from PhotoDisc. Used by permission.
Book design by James Satter

ISBN 0-8066-5158-X (Paperback)
ISBN 0-8066-5178-4 (Hardcover)

The paper used in this publication meets the minimum requirements of American National Standard for Information Sciences—Permanence of Paper for Printed Library Materials, ANSI Z329.48-1985. ♾ ™

Manufactured in the U.S.A.

08   07   06   05   04   1   2   3   4   5   6   7   8   9   10

Contents

Part IV
How Friendship Helps Our Spirit

This book is dedicated to my Dad,
H. Clark Bentall.

He was a great father.
He was also a man with many friends,
because he knew what it took
to be a good friend.

❖ ❖ ❖

Acknowledgments

This book is about friendship. It should therefore be no surprise that its creation was both inspired and assisted by many good friends. In fact, I am humbled by the realization of just how many friends upon whose shoulders this book rests.

The journey started with Chuck Ferguson, who first taught me about the kind of friendships Jesus had and created in me a thirst for something more in relationships.

Thanks, Chuck, for all the years of growth you sponsored, simply by unpacking the Scriptures so helpfully. Next, I wish to thank Bob and Carson for committing to me in friendship in such a remarkable way that this book could be a reflection of what we have learned about friendship together over the past fourteen years. It has been a privilege to have your support and encouragement to share our story.

I also want to thank Dr. Leighton Ford, who first suggested this project to Carson. We wouldn't have dreamt of doing this, without your stimulus.

Next, I would like to thank the handful of dedicated individuals who kindly read the early drafts of the manuscript, and gave critical and helpful suggestions. Specifically, John Weston, Dr. Stan Grenz, Murray Maisey, and Dr. James Houston. Without your input I wouldn't have known whether or not I even had a book worth completing.

I also want to thank Susan Martinuk for her tireless efforts and support as my primary editor. Thank you, Susan, for taking my ramblings and sifting them into something which is now much more coherent—and certainly more to the point!

Moreover, I wish to gratefully acknowledge Kent Hotaling, Doug Coe, Mark Powers, and all the other men from "The Fellowship," who helped me refine my thinking on this topic. Similarly, I want to thank Kevin Jenkins and his Harvard colleagues for inspiring me to reach higher in my quest for Godly friendship. Thanks also to Greg Gerrie for badgering me to complete this project. Had it not been for his encouragement, I might have folded my tent long ago.

Gratitude also goes to Larry Willard, who championed this book idea and helped connect me with Augsburg Books. Thanks for believing in me and for introducing me to Scott Tunseth. You have both been a terrific help to this neophyte author.

Finally, I want to list some of the men who, over the years beginning in kindergarten, have taught me about friendship. I have had many other friends, who are not listed here, but each of these—in a special way, over a special season—has marked my soul with special memories:

Dave Whyte, Alan Osborne, John Edmondson, Chris Bayne, Sean Lanigan, Donald Carson, Wayman Crosby, Dean Taylor, Mike Simms, Ron McCluskie, Bill Turner, Bruce Trevitt, Mark Boehmer, Barry Pettit, Doug MacInnis, Mark Bundy, Ric Carrick, Dave Phillips, Dave Miller, and Thane Stenner. I have been blessed with some of the best friends a man could ever ask for. Thanks, guys!

Preface

I suppose my first ideas about friendship came from watching my father interact with his friends. Dad had lots of good friends. In fact, I think my passion for friendship was really ignited by the observations I made as I came to terms with both the life—and the death—of my father. Let me tell you a bit about my Dad, H. Clark Bentall. His life experiences with friendship were remarkable. Let me also tell you a bit about my heritage, because it has helped shape my opinions on most things, including friendship.

For almost one hundred years, the Bentall family name has been synonymous with the construction of downtown Vancouver. My grandfather, Charles E. Bentall, first captured public attention in 1911, when he designed what was then the tallest building in the British Empire. Five years later, he acquired the Dominion Construction Company, a leading design/build company. He served as president of the corporation for forty years before passing the reins on to my father, Clark, the year that I was born. Between 1991 and 1998, I followed in their footsteps as president of Dominion.

Growing up, I watched my father as he developed the business into a fully integrated real estate development enterprise, which later became known as The Bentall Group. The firm expanded operations to cities across Canada and into California. At the zenith of his career, my father commanded an enterprise that had interests in real estate, construction, property management, mechanical and electrical contracting, interior design, and millwork manufacturing. Most notable, however, was his role in developing The Bentall Center.

Named after my grandfather Charles, this project boasts five office towers that are prominent features of the Vancouver skyline and today comprise the largest integrated office complex in Western Canada.

Nonetheless, my father's achievements are best summarized as follows:

- He was admired and respected by all of his employees, and during his tenure, The Bentall Group was voted one of the best one hundred companies to work for in Canada.
- He was awarded an honorary doctorate by the University of British Columbia where, fifty years earlier, he had earned his degree in engineering.
- He was always in demand as a corporate board member and, at one time, served simultaneously on seven boards, including those governing one of Canada's largest banks.
- He was awarded the Order of Canada in recognition of his outstanding community service.

Sadly, as my father aged, he was increasingly afflicted with Alzheimer's disease. After sixty years of continuous service to the family business, he was unable to travel to downtown Vancouver to enjoy lunch at The Vancouver Club, as had been his custom for more than thirty years. It seemed as though he had lost his status, both as an executive and as a community leader, almost overnight. To add to his burden, my mother, his wife of fifty-seven years, died quite unexpectedly from cancer. At the age of eighty, he had not only lost his loving partner, but he was also a stranger to the business to which he had devoted most of his life.

Suddenly his list of accomplishments didn't seem to matter much, nor did they bring any degree of comfort. It was during these darkest of times that I saw he still had two shining rays of light in his life—his faith in God and his circle of friends. I was inspired to realize that he had lived his life well by taking the time to create several close friendships that lasted, quite literally, for a lifetime.

After Mom died, Dad was alone. However, almost every Tuesday, for the next four years, Bruce Bayne came to share breakfast with my dad. Frank Burnham did the same every Thursday. These men stood by Dad as his physical condition deteriorated rapidly towards the end of his life. Even when he was no longer able to participate in lively discussions or go out for walks, they were there for him. He had virtually nothing to offer anyone. Yet, even in these circumstances, these men were there for my father. To me and to my entire family, their lasting faithfulness modeled the depths and the comfort of true friendship.

Introduction

Have you ever taken time to consider who is significant enough to you that they would faithfully see you through to the end of your life? Or might lovingly carry you as pallbearers when you die? Admittedly, most of us aren't at death's door, and hopefully won't be dying any time soon. But you might want to ask yourself: Do I have friends that will be there in times of loss, a marriage crisis, or a loss if you lose your physical or emotional health?

If you can honestly say that you have friends that meet these criteria, you are rare. Even if you do have good friends, two questions still remain:

1. *Are you currently investing time in your relationships?*
2. *Are you actively building friendships that will go the distance?*

If these questions are hard to answer, perhaps they will serve as an incentive for you to develop deeper friendships, or to take steps to further enhance already established friendships. If you don't currently have friends who might measure up to these high standards, then take comfort in knowing that, for many years, neither did I.

Like most men, my friendships were often determined in the same way as I select what to watch on TV, by incessantly clicking the remote. I typically flip through the channels, to see if there might be a show worth watching. Similarly, for much of my life, I was pretty haphazard when it came to finding and building friendships. This is not to say I didn't have good friends, because I did, but what I didn't have was a strategy for developing friendships.

How can we, as men, create meaningful friendships? How can we progress from hanging out with the guys after a game to a substantive friendship? Is it possible to be close enough to other men to want to confess one's fears or to discuss one's dreams? These are questions I had. Thankfully, I have discovered that if I want to have deep connections with other men, I can be intentional and purposeful in developing the kind of friendships that are not simply discovered, but actively sought after and built.

I have been actively seeking to build quality friendships with other men for more than twenty years. To say the least, my life is richer for it. To say more, required writing this book. When created with intent, and nurtured by the investment of time, our friendships can transform our lives: marriages can be strengthened, family ties enriched, careers enhanced, and spirits refreshed. This book provides a number of ways to initiate such friendships and describes, in depth, the life-changing benefits that stem from stepping out into the world of *intentional friendship.*

The benefits I see aren't speculative or theoretical. They're very real and, in many cases, are supported by the fifteen-year experience that I have had in sharing an intentional friendship with two men. One is Carson Pue, the international president of Arrow Leadership Ministries, and the other is Bob Kuhn, a prominent lawyer who has successfully argued cases before the Supreme Court of Canada. Over the course of the years, we have spurred each other on in making risky, yet highly positive career changes. We have helped each other to become better husbands and fathers, and we have led each other to grow in friendship with God. We have held each other accountable for how we live our lives and encouraged one another into ratcheting up our fitness levels. Carson, Bob and I are, in every sense of the word, true soul mates.

Each of us has made significant breakthroughs in recent years. All three of us have launched new careers. All of us have achieved fitness results that we never dreamt possible, and we each have had profound faith-enriching experiences. Were these coincidental? I don't think so. Typically, breakthroughs like we have enjoyed result from determination and effort. Yet these efforts have been multiplied and fortified by the prayer, courage, motivation, and support that have come from our friendships.

Our friendships have a transforming power that has profoundly affected the stories of each of our lives, and this is demonstrated in the following pages. More than twelve years ago, we three decided to take our friendship one step further. At that time, we drafted and signed an agreement that we called our "Covenant Partnership." It is rare, somewhat original, and perhaps even radical. However, it is not all that complicated. It is simply a written agreement that outlines our lifelong commitment to "be there" for each other. In it, we commit to eight specific promises:

- To affirm one another
- To be available to one another (in proper relation to our commitments to marriage and family)
- To pray with and for one another
- To be open with one another
- To be honest with one another
- To treat one another with sensitivity
- To keep our discussions confidential
- To be accountable to one another

The purpose of this book is to encourage readers to explore the many frontiers of friendship that exist and to be intentional about building relationships that will last and pay dividends in the years to come.

In *The Four Loves,* C. S. Lewis rightly states that friendship is the "least natural of loves, the least instinctive."[1] It goes against the natural grain of our world. We are driven out of necessity and instinct to invest time in earning money and being with family. While there may be no biological need for friendship, there is a very human need and desire for friendship. Still, with the demands of life, it often falls to the bottom of our priority list. Men should fight hard against this inclination by being intentional and purposeful in developing friendships.

I'm not talking about growing your network. Rather, I'm inviting you to join in an exciting journey toward transformational friendship, where men create and nurture enduring, meaningful relationships of mutual support. It may not be a well-worn trail, but it is one worth traveling. Come and join me in the pursuit of the exhilarating and largely unexplored frontier of lifelong, God-honoring friendships between men.

Part I

Why Friendship Matters

You may not want to admit it—or be prepared to do anything about it—but at some level, all men know that friendship matters. We can all recall going to a playground as young boys and feeling a strong desire to join in and play with the other kids. If we weren't welcomed by the group, it hurt. Now, at the office or while attending a conference, we realize that even as an adult, we have a need to belong . . . to have someone with whom we can interact.

In our adult lives, there seem to be an endless number of distractions, excuses, and imitations that attempt to fill this place in our lives. Chapter 1 examines some of these and demonstrates how they have created modern attitudes about friendship that fall far short of conveying its true and transformative nature. Some of these may actually prevent men from searching for, and experiencing, friendship. These deeply rooted and yet errant attitudes can be overcome by being intentional and purposeful in pursuing friendship. This is radically different than what is advocated and common in our society.

Chapter 2 provides a number of practical ways that men can use to both initiate and strengthen friendships. Surprisingly, you may find that you already know or use many of my suggestions. If so, then it's a matter of being intentional in applying them to specific relationships.

Finally, chapter 3 moves into the realm of creating a purpose for friendship. Common goals and a common vision can assist in moving a friendship forward in a positive direction. In particular, the concept of *covenant friendship* is defined and presented as the foundation for my friendship with Bob and Carson.

Chapter 1

A New View of Friendship

Have you ever thought that there could be more to friendship than watching a game, playing golf, or going out for a few drinks? Have you ever wanted or needed more from your relationships? Have you wished for a friend that you could honestly talk to about your career, your dreams for the future, or problems that you currently face? Wouldn't it be great to have a friend that will stand beside you, listen to you, affirm you, and support you?

If you uttered an inner yes to any of the above, you've just taken your first step toward adjusting your thoughts and expectations about friendships between men. Men's friendships can be deep, purposeful, and ultimately transformational. If you've picked up this book, I suspect there is a part of you that is already searching for the kind of friendship that makes a difference in how you live your life.

The idea of transformational friendship between men is radically different from our traditional understanding of relationships. It journeys beyond traditional notions, to uncharted territory where men are encouraged, loved unconditionally, held accountable, and are spiritually uplifted . . . by other men. It is different from the way friendship is portrayed in today's media and radically different from more popular philosophies that claim the "self" is self-sufficient. It's also radically different from the way we socialize boys as they individuate and mature, and different from the current cultural trend that may confuse male friendship with sexuality.

As you will see throughout this chapter, Western society does not encourage men to go out of their way to develop in-depth friendships with other men. That is one key reason why transformational friendship requires a paradigm shift in the way that all of us—men, women, and society at large—think about men and their most basic relational needs. As you read this book and begin to appreciate the full potential of male friendship, I encourage you to be a forerunner in your circle of relationships. You can choose to be the radical leader, the first to step beyond the usual bounds of friendship. You can be the one who will take your relationships with your male friends into fresh places, where men are transformed through affirmation, mutual support, and unconditional love. Add to these accountability and genuine encouragement, and you will have created friendships that will assist you to excel in all areas of your life.

Friendship can transform men. But before we see how that works in practice, we need to look at how culture may create our misconceptions of what male friendship is and what it can be.

How Transformational Friendship Is Radically Different

Transformational male friendship is not the norm in today's society. Let's take a look at a few ways popular culture clouds the picture.

Friendship As Portrayed in the Media

Most of us would agree that television, movies, and commercials don't offer particularly accurate portrayals of real life. This also holds true for their depiction of men and their friendships. Most entertainment limits friendship to a bunch of guys hanging out together, going to the bar, or watching a game. There may be nothing wrong with these things, but such images rarely portray male friendship as anything beyond superficial interaction. Beer commercials are classic examples of the purported simplicity of male bonding. In one commercial, a song pronounces that "It's guys night out," and then goes on to show men as mindless, ill-mannered sheep, heading to the bar, watching football on a big-screen TV, and ogling women. These types of ads reek of testosterone and probably sell lots of beer. But they also distort the concept of male friendship, reducing it to little more than a hedonistic night out on the town.

I played enough rugby and drank enough beer in my youth to understand that a night of drinking and partying is what many guys look forward to on the weekend. However, I also now realize that it's a pretty shallow imitation of the full potential of true male friendship.

Television sitcoms also tend to show men and their friendships in a less than glamorous light. Men are typically typecast as lazy and boorish, living to watch the games and trading competitive insults with each other. We all know guys like this, and in some cases their behavior is amusing. But as these images continue to fill the screen year after year, they create the false notion, especially for young men, that this is all there is to men's relationships and all that their friendships can be. By offering us these facile imitations of male friendship, the media invites society as a whole to give up on the expectation that male friendships can ever be more.

Society's Emphasis on Self-Sufficiency

In sharp contrast to the above, there is a strong popular cultural understanding of the male self that actually encourages isolation. The idea that men can and should be self-sufficient is commonly accepted as the key to survival. When I was growing up, the confident, masculine male was emulated in Western heroes like those portrayed by John Wayne or Marshal Matt Dillon in *Gunsmoke.* They were tough men who went the distance alone. They were protectors, yet seemingly uncommunicative and unconnected to family and relationships.

In today's business environment, we see that the assumption still exists that the strong, successful man is the man who gets the job done on his own. In our technology-crazed world, his job is to harness his laptop, saddle up his Blackberry or Palm Pilot, and charge into the day with his cell phone attached to his ear. Like a modern-day knight, he must battle for market share and for the next promotion. If someone happens to cross him along the way, the common strategic response is summarized in the words, "Don't get mad, get even." For real men, it's a dog-eat-dog, survival-of-the-fittest world. Who needs friends in this kind of world?

This "life as battleground" type of thinking hardly seems like the progressive mentality that one might expect at the dawn of the twenty-first century. Yet tough-minded, steely-eyed, self-sufficiency is typically presented to men as the basic game plan for success in career and in life.

But is the success of the individual based in reality or in cultural myth? Does any achievement really come from the efforts of just one person? We may struggle to achieve goals on our own, yet the moment we achieve anything significant, it becomes abundantly clear that we couldn't have possibly made it by ourselves. Even those who stand in the spotlight after receiving an Oscar thank a long list of supporters who made their success possible. Peter Legge is a successful businessman, author, and motivational speaker. He states, "It is almost impossible for anyone to succeed without the help, encouragement, and support of others."[1] But he also qualifies that by saying that men rarely acknowledge this fact. That is, despite an overall understanding that success requires others, the idea that we should be able to make it alone remains deeply engrained in our male psyche. To our own detriment, we continue to idolize individualism.

The Way Men Are Socialized in Western Culture

When I first started to tell others about my work on this book, I was struck by the response I got from women. Without exception, they were eager to get their hands on it, saying, "I want a copy for my husband; he could use some close friends." Perhaps this isn't surprising. While men seem to be less interested in friendship, women tend to more naturally understand its value. Therefore they are far more willing to take action that creates and sustains their friendships. In his book *Bowling Alone,* Robert Putnam states:

> Married or single, employed or not, women make 10–20 percent more long-distance calls to family and friends than men, are responsible for nearly three times as many greeting cards and gifts, and write two to four times as many personal letters as men. Women spend more time visiting with friends, though full-time work blurs this gender difference, by trimming friendship ties for both sexes. Keeping up with friends and relatives continues to be socially divided as women's work.... In short, women are more avid social capitalists than men.[2]

Friendship may seem like "women's work" to some men, but it doesn't have to be this way. If you think about it, most men have many friends while attending school or university. They may play sports together and then "cruise for chicks" together, as they get older. Yet Dave Phillips, a noted motivational speaker, world class athlete, and former Canadian national alpine freestyle ski team member, has observed that in North America "most men make no real close friends after high school." In fact, he believes that "after the age of 40, men typically have no close friends at all."[3]

What happens? Why is there such a substantially negative change in the social structures and attitudes of men as they grow older?

One author puts the blame squarely on the process of growing up.[4] It is inevitable that as men mature and move from education into the work force, the former emphasis on fun and friends shifts to one of succeeding in work and living. As they marry, they necessarily develop a new focus on marital and familial life. In essence, as men move through life stages, their priorities change.

On the surface, this reasoning holds true. But beneath it lies a deeper, cultural truth that is often ignored. That is, we have been raised by generations of men before us who had few close friends and who typically ignored (or feared to face) their need for true friendship. Perhaps because times were tougher, they felt the need to display a tough exterior, behind which they hid their true selves.

In earlier generations, I suspect that men had less discretionary time. Time with friends was probably more related to working together on the farm or on a community project. Out of necessity, our predecessors had to focus on making a living, and they worked long, hard days (like many of us still do) at jobs that mostly consisted of heavy, manual labor. Before microwaves, fast-food, and supermarkets, men were busy raising livestock or growing their own crops. They didn't have a coffee house or movie theater on every corner; a book or a guitar was considered to be sophisticated entertainment; and they didn't have television gurus to advise them on how to best display their emotions or maintain their relationships.

In this environment, friendships were forged out of the need for alliances, as men worked together to build homesteads, harvest crops, and provide for their families. For the most part, these relationships were not intensely personal nor geared to bringing out the best in each other. Today, men are, in a sense, raised to believe they must go it on their own, perpetuating the myth that security is not found in close relationships, but in solitude. Thus, men purposefully work to distance themselves from their emotional needs, as those around them frown on any who would dare to admit a need for support.

The high degree of mobility that is demanded by current economic realities also affects men's relationships. It used to be the norm for a man to take a job, put down roots, and build life in a single community. But now we gravitate to where the opportunities are, and this change in lifestyle and community has conspired to keep us from building long-term, quality friendships.

Even in small towns where everyone knew everybody else, life has become more private. The agrarian way of life has been replaced for many of us, with the complexities of urban living. Today, our busy schedules lead us to drive home from work, enter our garages via our remote controls, and slip, unnoticed by our neighbors, into our domestic enclaves.

Many of us crave privacy and are quite content to be at home rather than socialize with our neighbors. It isn't that we aren't interested in them, but we inevitably make choices as we build our workplace, business, and social networks. There's only so much we can do. No one can sustain an infinite number of acquaintances, so why try to add friendships with neighbors to an already overwhelming network?

The need for privacy in one's home may be justified. As a result of this kind of thinking, many of us live in homes that are relatively insular from our neighborhoods and communities.

Fear of Sexual Overtones

Perhaps the most disturbing factor that keeps men, especially young men, from pursuing in-depth male friendships today is the modern cultural inference that any close male relationship must have a sexual dimension. Discussions of male friendship are often confused, because close friendship between men is sometimes considered to be linked to sexuality, even if often only in jest.

It is important to recognize and affirm that men can have close, supportive and meaningful relationships that are wholesome and have nothing to do with sexuality. It would be tragic to allow current societal attitudes to intimidate us into believing that a hidden sexual agenda exists in all male friendship—when nothing could be further from the truth.

C. S. Lewis, Oxford university professor and one of the most lucid Christian thinkers of the last century, points out that, where homosexuality is concerned, "The very lack of evidence is treated as evidence."[5] That is, homosexuality has taken such a hold on our thoughts about male friendship that its very absence has now become proof that it *must* be present. He says assumed homosexuality is like an "invisible cat." There is no evidence that it exists and we can't see it. Yet, we presume it must be there simply because we have been told that invisible cats exist. Therefore, not seeing the cat supports the claim that it is there.

To be sure, our perceptions are now so colored that we see things that don't exist, and this misperception can keep men from developing healthy, purposeful friendships. Lewis concludes that those who have this misleading notion reveal the sad fact that they have never known true friendship. It would be sad, indeed, if a cultural preoccupation with homosexuality acted as a potential barrier to the development of male friendship. This is an area where, perhaps more than any other, it is critical that men think about meaningful friendships in a manner that is radically different from that of society.

Do Male Friendships Undermine Marriage?

Admittedly, sometimes men develop friendships at the expense of spending time with their spouses. However, it is vitally important to state bluntly that I am not encouraging men to pursue in-depth friendships that take time, energy, and resources inappropriately away from their marriages. The kind of purpose-ful friendship that I am advocating affirms marriage and seeks to help men become better husbands and better fathers.

Male friendship can actually reduce some of the emotional load that is typically borne by wives. Unfortunately, many men believe that marriage should provide all the intimacy and sup-port that they desire, and they seek to experience their full rela-tional completeness exclusively through marriage.

If we really think about it, we would probably conclude that it would be unfair that any one person should be expected to meet all of our needs single-handedly. In our work environment, we readily acknowledge that a team is required to get the job done. Corporations need marketing, finance, and operations. A championship football team needs a strong offense and a good defense, as well as specialty and role players. So why is it that so many of us have such unrealistic expectations of marriage? Why do we assume that our spouse will provide *everything* we need in terms of love, friendship, encouragement, spiritual guid-ance, wisdom, support, and intimacy?

The truth is that healthy relationships outside of marriage can prevent us from placing on our spouses the full burden of meeting the myriad of our intimacy and friendship needs. There-fore, we need to make room in our lives for relationships that provide emotional and relational support, so that we can be sus-tained and encouraged in building our marriages.

I am not in any way suggesting that transformational friend-ship be equated with a marriage relationship or that marriage should become one among several equal relationships. A man's first allegiance is to his wife and family. Some may argue that by placing time with your wife and children in proper priority there isn't enough time for other relationships. This may be true for some. But I am convinced that the greater problem is the ten-dency for married men to dump most of their relational needs at their wives' feet. The opposite tendency, and one which is just as harmful, is for men to live lonely lives that deny their relational needs. Neither of these makes for a full or happy life.

Given a group of close friends, we can complement and affirm our marriage relationships, as well as establish relational environments that are capable of developing and sustaining the strong fabric of interrelationships.

All Men Have a Desire
to Know Others and Be Known

While social factors have often conspired to discourage friendships between men, there is growing evidence that men are beginning to recognize their need for a deeper connection with both their own maleness and with other men. The emergence and popularity of male retreats in the 1980s, in both Christian and secular realms, declared that men are in need of recovering something integral to their well being. Men need to gather together to find mutual strength, encouragement, and accountability.

In 1990, University of Colorado football coach Bill McCartney provoked an overwhelming response from North American men when he created Promise Keepers, an organization geared to build up men of integrity by encouraging them to establish vital relationships with other men.[6] As tens of thousands of men gathered together in football stadiums, spiritual bonds were formed and men pledged to help each other keep their commitments to God, wives, and families.

In 1995, one million African American men gathered in Washington's National Mall to demonstrate strength and unity. They committed to "clean up their lives," "clean up their neighborhoods," "take responsibilities for their families," and "bring the spirit of God back into their lives." The Million Man March was led by Nation of Islam leader Louis Farrakhan, who urged men to band together and to be accountable to each other in keeping their pledges. Both of these mass movements for men display a yearning for something, and I am convinced that some of that something is the deep bond of male friendship.

Bill Hybels, the inspirational leader of Chicago's well-known Willow Creek Church, believes that all men long to know other men and to be known by them.[7] He says that men have four basic needs for companionship, which we innately long to have fulfilled:[8]

- to know and be known
- to love and be loved
- to celebrate and be celebrated
- to serve and be served

Many of us have never thought about life in terms of these needs. In fact, we are too busy doing things to even think about our most urgent needs, let alone needs as esoteric as being known by others. Maybe some of us would agree that we long to love and be loved, but even when this point is conceded, we usually limit our definition of love to something more transient—a love that comes and goes, that we're lucky to find, even for a while.

We are equally uncomfortable with the notion that friends, or anyone else, would want to celebrate us, except perhaps on our birthdays. The concept of being served or serving another is foreign to many of us as well, especially for men raised to be self-sufficient. It may be okay to be pampered at a fine restaurant or hotel and by service staff, but few of us would allow our friends to literally act as servers to us.

Yet when these four elements are combined (knowledge, love, celebration, and service), they create community, a team, a place of mutual strength and encouragement—the very thing that all men need, but seldom experience.

Vince Lombardi, the legendary coach of the Green Bay Packers, has observed that we all want to be closely allied with others in a winning cause, but winning only happens when team members care for each other. He said, "You've got to care for one another. Each player has to be thinking about the next guy. The difference between mediocrity and greatness is the feeling these players have for one another. Most people call it team spirit. When the players are imbued with that special feeling you know you have yourself a winning team."[9]

I have had the privilege of playing on championship rugby teams, both in high school and at university. Even as I think of it now, the exhilaration and sense of celebration that we experienced as a team after a victory still seems beyond description. The disappointment after a loss obviously didn't have that sense of exhilaration, yet the special bond between teammates was still there. As a team, we shared the victories and the defeats—together.

If we aren't part of a winning athletic team, then we want to be part of a corporate enterprise that's "shooting the lights out" or a volunteer organization that's truly making a difference. This desire to belong to, or be associated with, others in an enterprise of excellence reflects our need to connect with a greater vision or a worthy cause.

I experienced that "community" while serving on staff at a YMCA camp in my late teens.For four years, I instructed water-skiing at Keats Camps, located on a spectacular island off the Pacific Coast of British Columbia. Its beauty was awe inspiring, but perhaps even more remarkable was the sense of unity and purpose that I shared with fourteen other staff members. In this environment, quality friendships blossomed quite naturally. As leaders, we had the opportunity to share outdoor activities, music, and laughter with each other, as well as with the hundreds of children who spent the summer with us. As we helped the kids to discover the refreshing cool water of God's love, we also learned to love and care for each other, and some of us developed true and lasting friendships.

I've also enjoyed comparable experiences in my working career. On one occasion, I had the privilege of leading the executive team that developed a downtown office tower that today is the tallest building in the city of Winnipeg. It has also been regarded by many as architecturally superior to any other project in the city.

Later in my career, as president of Dominion Construction, I helped our firm secure a $100 million contract to build another notable structure, General Motors (GM) Place. With a seating capacity of 20,000, it serves as the home of the Vancouver Canucks and as a venue for other major entertainment events. Interestingly, GM Place was the largest project our company ever built in its illustrious eighty-year history.

However, as satisfying as these projects were, it was in some ways even more satisfying to be connected with the men and women who worked together to make these dreams come true.

Conclusion

As I look back over my life, I cherish these memories—the rugby teams, the camp, and the executive teams of which I played a part. All were exceptional. I felt that I "belonged" and that I was part of a group that was accomplishing something greater than any of us could have done on our own.

These experiences were significant and have helped shape my development as a person. But I have experienced something even more profound by building a few quality, friendships.

There is much uncharted territory in the realm of purposeful and transformational male friendship. However, these frontiers are worth exploring, and the rewards can be significant. The journey requires a certain amount of courage and a desire to look for a type of friendship that is radically different from what society conventionally advocates. Nonetheless, many areas of my life have been transformed and enriched through meaningful friendships, and I want to share my experience with you in the hope that you will be inspired to push further into the world of friendship.

A true friend is always loyal, and a brother is born to help in time of need.

—Proverbs 17:17, *The Living Bible*

Chapter 2

Making Friends on the Playground and at Harvard

Just after the conclusion of World War II, some of the world's most renowned leaders and dignitaries were invited to a formal dinner party to eat some of Europe's finest foods. At the table, an elegant and refined, yet relatively unknown British woman found herself seated between two of the most significant men of that era. On her one side was Mohandas Gandhi, the prime minister of India; on her other side was Winston Churchill, the prime minister of England.

One could hardly ask for a more scintillating pair of conversationalists. The next day, when the woman was asked what it was like to sit between these two world leaders, her poignant reply was revealing, "Churchill was fascinating! I have never met anyone who was more interesting!" In stark contrast, when describing Gandhi, she simply stated, "I have never met anyone who was more interested *in me.*"

Being a Friend Means Being Interested in Others

What do you do when you meet someone at a reception or dinner party? Do you try to be interesting? Or do you demonstrate an interest in them? Being aware of this distinction is the first step to understanding what it takes to build a friendship.

Being a friend begins with being interested in other people. Building relationships begins when we are other-centered rather than self-centered.

Think back to a time when you entered a new school or neighborhood and didn't know anyone—or even to the last business conference or social gathering that you attended. Did you notice that the best friendship builders were those who looked around for someone else who was standing alone, and then reached out to that person? Some people may reach out because of their own needs, where others may do so unselfishly. The end result is the same. The loneliness and awkward feelings melt away in the warmth of another.

Several years ago, I attended the Owner/President Program at Harvard Business School. The participants included owners, presidents, and CEOs from around the world. Their only common bond was a desire to be the best corporate leaders they could be.

It goes without saying that this was a highly intelligent and self-reliant group. As an experiment, I thought it would be interesting to get their insights and perspectives on friendship. A group of us met together over lunch to explore what it takes to build close friendships. It was fascinating how the thoughts on friendship that emerged from this sophisticated group of leaders at Harvard were so remarkably similar to those commonly found on an elementary school playground.

Consider the following insights that our group made about friendship, along with the corresponding friendship needs of children:

At Harvard	On the playground
A friend is someone who takes a risk with you by being vulnerable.	A friend is someone who shares his toys with you.
A friend is someone who takes initiative.	A friend is someone who invites you over to his house to play.
A friend is someone in whom you can confide.	A friend is someone to whom you can tell secrets.
A friend is someone for whom you want the best, and he wants the best for you.	A friend is one who cheers for you and someone for whom you can cheer.
A friend is someone to whom you can talk.	A friend is someone who listens to you.

Note that our needs for friendship don't change significantly, even as we get older, wiser, and more sophisticated. Neither does the idea that the ideal friend is one who is other-centered.

However, the concept of putting others first isn't intuitive. It involves a distinct choice on our part to reach out.

Being a Friend Requires Vulnerability

Friendship also involves taking risks, and most times that means being vulnerable. Many of us hesitate to be open wth others, since we have all been hurt, let down, or disappointed by people. Perhaps someone promised to meet us and then forgot, or someone promised to care for us and they didn't. Perhaps you thought you had a friend who would be there for life, yet after a period of time you drifted apart. The bottom line is that, at some point, each of us has been vulnerable in friendship, and hurt as a consequence.

In *The Four Loves,* C. S. Lewis warns that there are no assurances against heartbreak—either in love or in friendship. Protecting our hearts from hurt by locking them "safely in the coffin of selfishness" will keep them from being broken, but it will also change them. "In that casket—safe, dark, motionless, airless—it will change. It will not be broken; it will become unbreakable, impenetrable, irredeemable."[1] The choice to befriend others and to be vulnerable is ours. The problem is we too often make that choice by considering the negative consequences that *might* result from being vulnerable, rather than thinking about the positive implications to our psychological well-being that will be our reward if we choose to open our hearts to others.

Christy, my eldest daughter, came to understand this in a delightful way during her high school graduation year. She and her friends attended a relatively small, tight-knit, strong-spirited school. As graduation approached, they began to realize they would soon be taking different paths in life and might never all be together again. They were quite apprehensive about ending this phase of their lives until one of them came across the following phrase: "Don't cry because it's over, but rather smile because it happened." Indeed, by adopting this attitude, they chose to draw closer together in their final weeks rather than to drift apart in an attempt to diminish the feeling of loss that was inevitable. Those who adopted this approach were able to celebrate and savor their remaining time together.

The Law of Reciprocity

Peter Legge, as mentioned before, is an internationally recognized motivational speaker. He is also an author, publisher of *BC Business* magazine, and president of Canada Wide Magazines, Ltd. Among all these distinctions however, Peter is probably best known as a "friend maker." He is constantly looking to encourage and support those around him. As a result, those of us who he counts among his close friends consider ourselves fortunate. When speaking to groups, he often refers to the "law of Reciprocity,"[2] which states very simply that we will all reap what we sow. Let's think about this in terms of friendship.

One of my passions in life is slalom water skiing. For five years now, I have been traveling to Boca Raton, Florida, to train several times each winter. In the summer, I compete in numerous tournaments in the Pacific Northwest and across western Canada. Each fall, I travel with friends to California, where we ski at some event sites.

I began competing in this sport when I was approaching forty years of age, and it has been a thrill for me to learn and develop athletically at this age. However, as all water skiers know, water skiing is not a solitary sport. You must rely on someone to drive the boat and on someone else to crew or "spot" for you. (This essentially involves watching the skier and telling the pilot when the skier falls.)

One of my training partners for the past several years has been Ric Carrick. We often train two days per week from 7 to 9 A.M. For me, this means getting up at 5 A.M. to eat breakfast, drive one hour to the lake, and have the boat ready to go by 7 A.M. Rain or shine, Ric has always been there. He knows that if he drives for me, I will drive for him. It's a simple bargain, and a practical demonstration of the law of reciprocity in its most basic form.

Ric is a gifted athlete who has participated in many sports. As a result, he has suffered five concussions in separate sporting accidents. Now he suffers from frequent migraine headaches.

Unfortunately, these aren't just pop-an-aspirin-and-it-will-all-be-better type of headaches. The fact is that they can be so debilitating that he needs to place a blanket over his head to shield his eyes from light and to prevent the pain from becoming unbearable. Obviously, when Ric is feeling this way, he is not able to ski.

One morning, he called at 5:45 A.M. to say that a migraine was coming on. He was going to park his car at the side of the road and would phone me within forty-five minutes to update me on his condition. Sure enough, he called within the hour to let me know he was on his way. He couldn't ski, but was still willing to drive the boat. Time after time, Ric has demonstrated his commitment to be there for me, even when migraines, torn muscles, or even head colds would have caused less-dedicated friends to cancel.

How does his commitment to me relate to the law of reciprocity? Several weeks after this migraine episode, I felt that I had been skiing a lot and I wanted a day off. That same day, Ric had a chance to get some extra tow time on the water and asked if I would help him out. Despite the fact that I couldn't ski and had other plans, my first thought was, "After all Ric has done for me, how can I refuse to help?" So I adjusted my plans to accommodate his request. The law of reciprocity compelled me to be there for him even when I had other things I would rather do. It is a powerful principle that can be a practical foundation for building and sustaining all friendships.

I must hasten to add that this law goes beyond the concept of "he did something for me so, therefore, I owe him." Obviously, there can be a subtle keeping of score in friendships. However, the difference is in the attitude that a good friend has. In friendship, the attitude moves beyond "owing" and makes us *want* to do something for the other. As such, it reflects a true desire to honor a friend, not an obligation to pay up.

The Golden Rule

Another, more familiar principle that has great application in building friendships is the golden rule, Do unto others as you would have them do unto you.

In raising our four children, I have sometimes been called upon to help them settle their disagreements. In doing so, I typically ask them what the golden rule says about how they should be treating each other. Because we have gone over it many times, the kids now reply (perhaps with a bit of an edge), "The same way I want to be treated!" Once we get past this routine response, I ask them how the golden rule would apply to the present situation. In almost every case, they know how to apply the rule.

It's simple and profound advice: treat others as you want to be treated. In so doing, you will have discovered a great way to begin building friendships.

The Business Friendship

When prioritizing work time, most men tend to relegate friendship to the bottom of the list. The currency of the working world doesn't put much value on anything other than goals achieved and money made. Consequently, many men don't actively pursue friendship on the job. However, most of us have an established "network" of business contacts. If we want to "do lunch" with someone, we usually have a reason or an agenda. We look to these contacts to help us directly or to introduce us to other people. We may see some as a prospect for our business, or perhaps we owe them lunch because they helped us with a project that we were working on last month.

This utilitarian approach to friendships among men is a barrier to developing relationships with greater meaning. We may even believe that we are already experiencing the very best that friendship has to offer, simply because our luncheon schedules are full.

Unfortunately, by itself, the business friendship doesn't fulfill our deepest need to connect to other men and establish meaningful friendships. This is not to say that our work environment or a business lunch cannot act to initiate friendships that, over time, can become progressively more personal and supportive. In fact, this is an easy way for men to start friendships, and I would encourage you to take time this week to invite someone to "do lunch," for no other reason than for the sake of friendship.

Starting a Purposeful and Intentional Friendship

In my younger days, I didn't have particularly close friendships with other guys. This became painfully apparent when my wife and I were dating. During a romantic dinner, I told her that I loved her and then raised the subject of marriage, in a way that might allow me to see what she thought about it.

I then said, "Alison, if we were to decide to get married, I wouldn't know who to invite to be my best man." As those words came off my lips, I knew they revealed a deep truth about my lack of friendships with other men. Although I had scores of acquaintances from high school, university, rugby, and church, there were very few whom I could call friends. To use business terms, all I had was a pretty good network.

But if one day Alison and I were to walk down the aisle together, I wanted to have some real friends standing at the altar beside me. So, that night, I consciously made a commitment to begin building relationships with other men. I first made a list of ten or twelve men whom I already knew and who were, in my view, candidates for meaningful friendship. Alison and I then looked over the list together. We chose two guys (Mike and Dean) for me to approach to determine if they were interested in developing a deeper relationship with me. I followed through, and asked each guy if he was willing to work purposefully and intentionally at developing a closer friendship. I'm sure I was clumsy in my explanation, but somehow they got the message and, much to my surprise, I received a positive response from both of them.

Mike and I had first met several years earlier at a summer camp while we were both trying to "tidy" a ski boat. The ropes and boat fenders were not stowed in a manner that either of us felt was truly shipshape. Oddly enough, this common perspective brought about an instant connection. Just like Jerry on *Seinfeld,* we were both obsessively fastidious about neatness and quickly realized that we were alike in a way that might have quickly made others insane. I told Mike, right then and there, that he'd be the kind of guy I could share an apartment with.

After all, it's always best to keep the neat freaks together under one roof!

As it turned out, Mike and three others were looking for a fifth roommate to help share the cost of a house for the next year at university. Mike invited me to join them, and while sharing responsibilities for meal preparations and house cleaning, Mike and I built a close friendship.

My relationship with Dean also went back to my university days, as we worked together at a local restaurant. It was Dean who first gave me the idea of trying my skill at waiting tables. In fact, without his influence, I probably wouldn't have had the great experiences working Friday and Saturday nights serving prime rib.

Happily, a few years later, Mike served as the head usher at my wedding to Alison. Dean was there as my best man. (In a surprising but rewarding twist, I also stood as the best man at Dean's wedding when he married my wife's sister, Kathy!) Mike now lives in Australia and Dean in Southern California, but we all keep in touch, and something from that special season in our lives still lingers today.

The key to these friendships was that each of us was committed to making an investment in the relationship. Mike, Dean, and I didn't leave the growth of our friendship to chance. We made the decision to be purposeful about establishing meaningful friendships, and as a result we experienced significant relationships that provided support and strength as we journeyed through our twenties.

At that time, our friendship was radically different from our other friendships for the following reasons:

1. We talked about our relationship. Most friends enjoy doing things together, but rarely or never talk about how the friendship is going or how they can encourage or assist each other.

2. We were purposeful friends. In other words, we were proactive in building and bettering our relationships.

3. We made time together a priority. We didn't meet every week or always take part in the same activities. But we made a point of scheduling time for each other and scheduling other activities *around* this time together, rather than trying to squeeze our friendship into an overly full schedule.

4. We talked about goals that we had for our lives and careers, and offered input to each other, as well as support.

5. We prayed for each other, talked to each other about our spiritual growth, and endeavored to help one another in our spiritual walks with God.

Conclusion

This wasn't rocket science, although I was slowly becoming aware that there was more to "hanging out with the guys" than I had ever imagined. I realized that being together with other guys who shared my values gave me energy. It also gave me encouragement and insight, as daily challenges were discussed and as we problem-solved together. Purposefully and intentionally building friendships with other men may sound a bit revolutionary (or perhaps even odd) to some, but it leads to a life that can be transformed.

A man of many friends comes to ruin,
but there is a friend who sticks closer than
a brother.

—Proverbs 18:24

Chapter 3

Exploring Levels of Friendship

Accountability is critical to a healthy life and is an important area where friends can readily assist one another. It's easy for me to say this now. When the concept of accountability first presented itself to me almost twenty years ago though, I had no idea of what I was getting into nor how dramatically this one word would transform my friendships and my life.

In 1986, I was working at the Vancouver-based head office of the Bentall Group. Bob Kuhn was a lawyer who worked for our company, and although we knew each other as working associates, we had never considered each other to be particularly close friends.

One day, Bob had just finished a luncheon meeting, where the conversation had turned to a mutually known public figure whose life had recently fallen apart because of his unwise choices. Apparently, that spurred Bob on to wonder what would prevent someone like me from having the same experience.

Motivated more by curiosity than anything else, he poked his head out the door of his office and bluntly asked me, "Who are you accountable to?" Frankly, I didn't even know how to respond to this brash inquiry. So, believing that the best defense is a good offense, I attempted to turn the tables on him by saying, rather combatively, "No one. Why? Do you want me to be accountable to you?"

Bob wasn't certain that the heir apparent in a prominent family company would ever have experienced something that most people take for granted—that is, living and working under another's authority. In fact, he wondered if I had ever felt really accountable to anyone during my entire life.

At the time, he had no clue about the significance of his question or to where it would lead. Purportedly, he thought the question rhetorical and never dreamt that I would respond honestly, let alone be interested in exploring the idea of accountability. To his surprise—and probably my own as well—I agreed to talk more about it with him over breakfast the next week.

Exploring Friendship through Accountability

The more I thought about it, the more enthusiastic I was about the possibility of a relationship based on accountability. Prior to our meeting, I even took the time to pull together some related notes and articles that I had gathered during the past few years. For example, I had heard that Benjamin Franklin created a list of thirteen shortcomings in his character and then devoted his attention, each week, to working on one of these areas. With this in mind, over a fifty-two week period, he focused on each concern four times during the year, making a concentrated effort to eradicate his known faults and thereby improve his quality of life.

I thought about some specific behaviors that I wanted to change and created a list of weaknesses to show to Bob. I then told him the Benjamin Franklin story. He liked the idea, and then pointed out that I had an obvious problem with math (I had listed only twelve flaws). If we were going to be working together, he said I would have to list at least one other weakness. I readily conceded that this would be easy to do.

Some of these shortcomings reflected life-long habits that I had needed and wanted to change for a long time. Things such as, "I don't spend enough time with my wife, Alison," or "I tend to be critical," and "I give in to anger." They're typical faults that are common to many men. But despite my best efforts, I hadn't been able to overcome them on my own. As I confessed my inability to master these areas, I basically invited Bob to come alongside and encourage me.

For the next several months, Bob and I met each Wednesday morning to talk about how we were progressing in our lives. I gave Bob license to hold me accountable to working on one of these specific character flaws each week.

Perhaps you find yourself trapped in negative behavioral patterns, yet don't have the necessary perspective to know how to change or the motivation to accomplish change. A friend can offer a new and different perspective that can help all of us to honestly see what our lives are and what they can ultimately be.

Ironically, sharing our faults is a great first step toward building a meaningful relationship. As Bob assisted me in tackling my weaknesses, I was able to help him with his priorities. At the time, he was a volunteer board member with nine organizations and was either the chairman or one of the founders of several. As such, he was overwhelmed with all these responsibilities, particularly when combined with his law practice and the demands of a young, growing family. Since I wasn't emotionally or professionally involved, I found it relatively easy to ask, "If you could only choose three boards for active involvement, which ones would you choose?" After some thought, Bob was able to list the three that he felt were most important and that he felt the greatest need to support. By the next day, Bob had sent off six letters of resignation. He then happily advised me that he no longer was feeling overwhelmed by his commitments.

Sharing weaknesses and supporting each other was obviously beneficial to us both, yet we also realized that our friendship needed another dimension, as Bob describes:

After four plus years of exploring accountability in relationship with David, there appeared a number of weaknesses. Ironically, these tended to focus on the ways David and I were alike. We were both immersed in the business community, with a shared propensity for lists and accomplishments, challenges, and victories, and for climbing the corporate ladder, regardless of which wall it was leaning against. We both felt something was missing but were unclear what. Several times during our discussions, we had mulled over the possibility of bringing others into our mutual commitment, as ill-defined as it was then. It was just that the right person or circumstance never seemed to come along. David was keen on adding a more "spiritual dimension," perhaps recognizing our lack of maturity in that area of our lives. We had tried a more structured approach to spiritual development, but neither of us was able to gain much perspective from following some written prescription or book for spiritual maturity.

Exploring Friendship through Bible Study and Prayer

I sat in church one Sunday morning listening to a message by Carson Pue, a good friend whom I had met fifteen years earlier when we had lived in the same college dorm. As I listened, I began to think about how great it would be to renew my relationship with Carson and to have his insight in deepening my spiritual understanding, as well as his help in resolving issues related to my faith. He has a pastor's heart and a great sense of humor, both of which are tremendous assets in any relationship.

Carson and Bob weren't close friends, but they did know each other; Bob served as a deacon at the same church where Carson served as an associate pastor. I later talked to Bob and suggested that we invite Carson to assist us with some spiritual study to augment our attempts at growth and accountability in other areas. I'll leave it to Bob to pass on his unique perspective as our relationship took on this new dimension—and a new friend:

> *Bob:* I must admit that I initially perceived Carson's entry into our friendship as somewhat threatening. He and David, and their wives, were friends from way back, and I initially saw this as a recipe for disaster (perhaps replaying the tapes in my head from high school days when there could only be one "best friend").
>
> But it soon became apparent that this affable and prone-to-laughter pastor could not only contribute to our Christian resource building but also provide a wealth of perspective in other areas. It was then that we began to be more serious about the need to make a covenant. We saw a tremendous need for a strong commitment if we were going to grow, share at a deep level about our life's journey, and be willing to take risks with each other that might well shake our respective comfort levels in a serious way. The addition of a third member was the

impetus we needed to take it more seriously and to protect the level of commitment and ourselves in the process.

Maybe it was just the insecurity of three guys wanting something different than we saw out there; something more permanent, safer, stronger, and better. We wanted a friendship that reflected real commitment, despite what life might throw at us (or what we might throw at each other). Despite strong disavowals, we had seen many of our friends, acquaintances, and business associates stumble in their marriages, struggle with parenting, fail to meet the overwhelming challenges of careers, face health crises, and, perhaps most frightening, lose sight of the spiritual dimension of their lives. So perhaps it was fear that led us to talk about a life-long covenant relationship—one that we could count on when it was most needed.

We had heard about covenant friendships between men who wanted to live lives worthy of Christ's call on them. The more we explored the idea, the more it made sense. Why couldn't we commit for the long run? Perhaps we were naïve as to what it all meant, but like a marriage, it is only in living it out that we experience its depth and test its strength. So we committed to each other in a covenant, and, at times, it has been that decision that has kept us true to the original ideas of accountability and mutual support that forged this relationship.

I'm not exactly sure how we initially decided to create a covenant friendship. Carson thinks it was his idea, and I think it was Bob's idea. In any case, somehow, some way, we decided to formalize this friendship commitment to one another. Although it meant that our relationship was about to take another step forward, my first reaction to the idea was fear. What would it mean to commit to these guys—and what exactly was a covenant anyway?

Exploring Friendship through a Covenant

The dictionary says that a covenant is a promise. In the Old Testament, God made a covenant with the people of Israel when he promised to be their God and asked them, in return, to promise to be faithful to him.

We were familiar with the Old Testament story of David and Jonathan, who created a covenant of friendship through their promise to love and care for each other. This is one of the most profound and significant friendships ever recorded. It is easy to assume that Jonathan, a prince and heir to the throne of Israel, and David, a common shepherd boy, would have little in common that could be used as a foundation for friendship. In fact, you could say that their friendship first had to bridge a huge gap in social status, much like the proverbial prince and pauper. Even more amazingly, their friendship had to successfully bridge the harsh reality that God had chosen David to be the next king of Israel, rather than Jonathan, the heir apparent.

It sounds more like a soap opera than the beginnings of a spiritual friendship. Yet, the Bible says that their souls were "knit together" in friendship and that "Jonathan's soul became closely bound to David's, and Jonathan came to love him as his own soul." They agreed to become lifelong friends and made a "covenant" to symbolize their commitment to each other. To seal this oath, Jonathan gave David all the symbols of his royal heritage— his robe, his sword, his bow, and his belt (1 Samuel 18:1-4).

Jonathan's father, King Saul, became jealous of David, who had not only gained his son's friendship but was also a successful warrior who had won great popularity among the people of Israel. Hence, it wasn't long before Saul determined that David was a threat to his leadership and he began plotting to kill him. When Jonathan heard of these plans, he warned David to flee for his life. Their friendship, although preserved in spirit, became one of distance so that David could live.

The Bible makes it clear that David and Jonathan's friendship is one of magnanimous loyalty. According to David Benner, "we see it [their friendship] expressed in acts of loyalty, enormous risk taking, tender devotion and, ultimately, a covenant of eternal friendship sworn in the name of the Lord and binding on their descendants for all time."[1] In essence, they reinforced their commitment to each other by their actions and by their sworn commitment to honor and protect each other, despite the years, the miles, and the murderous tension between Saul and David.

Years later, after Jonathan had been killed, David was faithful to his covenant regarding their descendants. He honored their friendship by taking in and caring for Jonathan's only surviving offspring, a disabled son named Mephibosheth, who was invited to eat at David's table for the rest of his life.

David and Jonathan's backgrounds could not have been more disimilar, yet they still committed themselves to a life-long friendship. Like them, the three of us have diverse backgrounds, careers, and interests. Professionally, Bob is a lawyer, Carson a pastor and, at the time we established our covenant, I was a corporate executive. As for personal interests, Carson is musically talented and has played guitar and sung on the coffee-house circuit. Bob has a gift for launching new charities whenever he identifies a need, and he loves to read legal journals in his spare time. I can't carry a tune in a bucket, and my eyes would instantly glaze over if I tried to read the latest in case law. I am passionate about fitness and sports and am the most likely to dream up some wild activity for us to try. (As far as I'm concerned, swimming in the ocean in the middle of September, running at 5 A.M., or going sailing are all viable options when our covenant group meets.) But as we considered our own disparate hobbies and careers, we were inspired by the strength of the friendship bond that David and Jonathan sustained, despite their obvious differences and the incredible challenges they faced.

I remained concerned about the term of this proposed covenant and asked what would happen if one of the others moved away. Carson challenged this by saying, "If one of my siblings were to move away, that would not change the reality that they were my family." In the same way, he suggested that nothing prevented our friendship covenant from being a lifetime commitment. David and Jonathan were separated for much of their lives, and I doubt that they had an agreement to meet each week. Yet despite the distance (and their inability to overcome it using the modern technology that today we take for granted), their commitment remained intact. And so we determined, too, that once a brother, always a brother, no matter where any of us might wander.

After several weeks of discussion and prayer, several drafts, and even a few arguments, we signed a formal, eight-point contract that essentially bound us to support and encourage one another, as brothers, for life.

In a metropolitan area like Vancouver, geographical separations are almost a given. To be honest, the distance between areas of the city can make it more difficult to enjoy the benefits of our covenant, and sometimes living an hour away from the other two makes me feel a bit left out. Still, we continue to work at finding ways to get together and support each other and, over time, our covenant has successfully spanned geography.

In doing so, we have often been inspired by a good friend of mine, Kevin Jenkins. He has a covenant friendship with three men whom he met while attending Harvard Business School. These four men live in different cities across North America, yet they speak monthly via a telephone conference call, and their families routinely take vacations together during the summer. The miles clearly don't prevent them from having deep and ongoing, mutually supportive relationships. Their decision to spend holidays together has also prompted Carson, Bob, and me to plan vacations together more often with our families.

Why a Covenant?

I know that the idea of a formal, signed covenant may initially sound overwhelming and intimidating. But I'm convinced that understanding the following benefits of a covenant relationship will enhance any friendship:

1. A covenant provides the clarity and purpose that allows individuals to solidify relationships. We wanted to be supportive of each other and to grow old together. Typically, there is no certainty or expectation that friends will be there for each other over the long haul. Relationships by their very nature are fluid and, in an effort to combat this, we chose to create something that provided both clarity and assurance regarding our future expectations. Think about how you would feel if you had a job that was up for review at the end of every day or every week. Obviously, your sense of security is enhanced when you are hired on a long-term basis, whether it be a month, a year, or even longer. Similarly, a covenant offers us the security of

knowing that not only are we cared for today, but that we will also be cared for tomorrow.

For the most part, people are willing to be vulnerable only to the degree that they feel safe. A covenant creates a long-term safe place where we are free to share our lives, to experience meaningful exchanges and the genuine caring of friends. A written covenant, which we can always refer to, gives us a common understanding and vision to build a relationship that will last a lifetime.

2. A covenant provides ceremony, and relationships are always strengthened by ritual or ceremony. The traditions of shaking hands or signing a contract mark a confirmation of two parties' intentions when they enter into a business arrangement. Similarly, speaking vows and exchanging rings give substance to a wedding ceremony. Each of these simple acts adds strength and a sense of permanence to our commitments. Obviously not all contracts nor all marriages are honored, but this doesn't diminish their importance of making covenants. In fact, I would argue that this all-too-common reality of individuals not carrying through with their intentions underscores the need for each of us to reexamine what it takes to make and keep our promises. Rather than being put off by the failures of others to keep covenants, we can *choose* to let this spur us on to keep our commitments so that we won't be the ones disappointing others.

Conclusion

My journey into deep and intentional friendship started more than twenty years ago. For more than a dozen years, that journey has included a covenant relationship with two great guys, Carson and Bob. We share a life-long commitment to support each other, and I want to use examples from our friendship to encourage others to think about the benefits of a purposeful and lasting friendship. Throughout this book, I hope to open a window for you through which you can recognize—and begin to develop the kinds of relationships that can significantly enhance your life experience.

*Jonathan made a covenant with David because
he loved him as himself. . . . Then Jonathan said to
David , . . . "Show me unfailing kindness like that
of the Lord as long as I live," . . . and Jonathan had
David reaffirm his oath . . . because he loved him
as he loved himself.*

—1 Samuel 18:3; 20:12, 14a, 17, NIV

Part II

How Friendship Works

As described in the previous chapter, I share a unique friendship with Carson Pue and Bob Kuhn. It is undergirded by a written, lifetime covenant of mutual support in which we commit to eight specific promises: *to affirm* one another, *to be available* to one another (in proper relation to our commitments to marriage and family), *to pray* with and for each other, and *to be open* with each other. In addition, we commit to relate to each other *in honesty, sensitivity,* and *confidentiality.* Lastly, we choose *to be accountable* to each other. The next eight chapters explore some of our interactions related to these specific areas and illustrate how our friendship has influenced us as we strive to achieve our individual goals.

Not everyone will want to put their expectations for friendship in writing, and I am not necessarily advocating that you do so. But every man shares a common need for support and encouragement in each of the areas that are mentioned in our friendship covenant. As a result, any one (or more) of these can serve as a fundamental building block for men to develop meaningful relationships and to establish a safe environment where friendship can thrive. The following section describes in detail how friendship can challenge and transform those in covenant friendship in these eight areas.

Chapter 4

What Can We Do about Criticism?

Covenant of Affirmation: There is nothing you have done or will do that will make me stop loving you. I may not agree with your actions, but I will love you as a person and do all I can to hold you up in God's affirming love.

Every day, we are bombarded by negative, critical, and judgmental language. Statements like "You fool," "You're hopeless," or "That will never work in a million years" are casually tossed out in conversation. Whether spoken in jest and without proper thought or with intention, these comments can still result in bruised egos. Ironically, the remarks that undermine our confidence most are all too often uttered by those closest to us, while those who find the most to appreciate in us are usually those who don't know us as well.[1] The continuous onslaught of criticism and negativity can be debilitating and, for many, make it almost impossible to maintain a healthy sense of self-esteem. It's no wonder that so much of our self-talk is cluttered with self-defeating, negative thinking.

Criticism can be overcome, but it isn't easy. The best way to overcome the negative impact of words is to fight back with positive words. That's why, in our covenant, we have committed to consciously affirm each other. In so doing, we build each other's confidence and provide mutual support.

Criticism and Affirmation

Does this mean that we simply offer each other trite words of praise? I would hope not. Instead, it means that I have two men who are committed to helping me believe the best about myself and who I am. This is vital, because we all have a choice about how we see ourselves, and we make and remake that choice hundreds of times each day. Each of these choices is profoundly affected by the words that are spoken to us and about us.

I grew up in a family where athleticism was rarely practiced or encouraged. Consequently, I grew up thinking of myself as a nonathlete. But from the time I was in kindergarten until the time I finished high school, my best friend, Dave Whyte, was a star athlete who made a point of encouraging me to participate in a variety of sports. As a result, I learned to play soccer, rugby, and basketball.

Despite my best efforts, basketball didn't come easily to me. I remember standing under the hoop one day after school, trying to do a left-handed layup. I had recently mastered the right-handed layup, but consistently making left-handed layups was a real challenge. For some reason, I simply couldn't get my right knee to go up at the same time as my left hand.

There I stood, feeling like a total klutz, when Don McCormick, the senior-team basketball coach, called out, "What are you doing, Bentall?" My heart sank. I thought I had been caught looking totally uncoordinated out on the basketball court! After I explained what I was trying to do, he nonchalantly said, "If you want to practice with the senior team sometime, you'd be welcome to join us. Just let me know."

I felt even worse. Not only had I been embarrassed in failing to learn a basic skill, now the senior team coach was mocking me—or so I thought. That is, I immediately interpreted his comments as a negative, critical judgment of my ability. My self-esteem was so fragile that this off-handed comment by a person of authority was sufficient to destroy any hopes I had of playing basketball in the future. As a consequence, I decided to quit as soon as the season was over.

But the story doesn't end there. Several years later, I once again came face to face with Don McCormick. While reminiscing about high school basketball, Don asked me why I had never accepted his invitation to play with the senior team. I was stunned that he even remembered the conversation and explained to him that I had thought he was making fun of me. He then astonished me by stating that, quite to the contrary, "I saw such talent and promise in you that I was genuinely asking you to come and play with the senior basketball team, even though you were two years younger than most of the other players."

Wow! I had been so conditioned to accept any comments on my athletic abilities as criticism that I had taken positive comments—and a unique invitation—as a negative reflection on my abilities. As I think back on it, I still regret this missed opportunity.

Most of us think we are competent at least in some areas—and this inner feeling gives us a certain amount of self-confidence. John Gray, author of the popular book *Men Are from Mars, Women Are from Venus,* is quite accurate when he states that a man's "greatest fear is that he is not good enough or that he is incompetent."[2] This constant fear causes many men to live in a confused state of mind, where we begin to look for criticism, even in the midst of praise (just like I did with my basketball coach).

Similarly, when I shared a house with friends during my university days, I was nicknamed "The Armadillo." It was appropriate since anytime someone even looked in my direction, I'd be the first to say, "I didn't do it!" and then pull my head into my shell to avoid confrontation or criticism. Fortunately, as I have matured through the years and with the support of friends who affirm me, I am becoming better able to deal with such insecurities.

When Nate Adams[3] wrote a magazine article about his wife's desire for affirmation, he recounted an incident when she had asked him whether she should wear a red or black dress to a special event they were attending that evening. At first, he actually thought that she wanted his advice. Soon however, he realized that she was perfectly capable of making the decision about a dress. Instead, she was asking him for affirmation. She had come to him, perhaps feeling slightly insecure about the upcoming dinner, and had wanted him to say she'd look great in either dress. Some of you may think that this is manipulative, but I think her actions are understandable, and normal. She needed affirmation that evening, as we all do, from time to time.

Affirmation provides motivation for improvement, so it makes sense that successful athletes rely on coaching and that a successful coach affirms his athletes. Both novice and professional athletes need to know that they are making progress—and that comes from encouragement and affirmation. There are certainly other techniques that a coach may use, but by far the most effective ones are laced with positive reinforcement. John Wooden, perhaps the most successful coach in NCAA basketball history, says, "One of the most powerful motivating tools you can use is the pat on the back."[4]

Wooden goes on to say that affirmation is significant in every aspect of our lives, whether in leading a team to a national basketball championship or in offering advice as a parent. Mark Twain wasn't an athlete, yet he acknowledged the life-giving power of words for all of us when he wrote, "I can live for two months on a good compliment." We all need more affirmation than we typically receive, and our friends can, and should be, our best cheerleaders.

Provide Proper Rewards

Similarly, in business the results that we achieve are usually directly related to the rewards that we give—or get. Dr. Aubrey Daniels is a pioneer in applying the principles of behavioral psychology to the workplace and consults with a number of *Fortune 500* companies on management and human performance issues. His book *Bringing Out the Best in People* discusses how to effectively motivate those who work for you. In it, he states that "negative reinforcement can start a poor performer moving in the right direction, but only positive reinforcement can keep that person going."[5]

Daniels also claims that if you are experiencing poor results with a corporation, division, or person, you should examine the rewards that you are giving them. That is, if you look beneath the surface, you will find that you are rewarding the very behavior you are getting. So if you want to change the behavior or the performance, then you need to change the rewards.

When I first read about this, I was unwilling to accept it. I was particularly opposed to the notion since, at the time, there was a particular division of our company that was not performing to its potential. I was loath to believe that their poor performance was due to my rewarding them inappropriately.

However, as I studied the situation and thought more about this principle, I began to see a different picture emerge. I soon realized that the promotions and perks that went to that division had little to do with the kind of success we were seeking. More specifically, it became apparent we were only rewarding design excellence, rather than profitability. No wonder we couldn't get our staff to change their behavior; we were inadvertently rewarding the very behaviors we didn't want.

The application of providing proper rewards also holds true for friendship. Bob, Carson, and I have candidly spoken with each other about the changes we want to affect in our behaviors, our goals for marriage and family, and our dreams for the future. In doing so, we each invited the others' input to help us—not just by pointing out areas to adjust but also by pointing out the good and the successes. That is, in influencing one another's behaviors, wise friends don't just focus on the bad parts or mistakes; but rather, they are "always looking harder for the good" that they can affirm.[6]

For example, I want to love my wife and children more consistently, and make it a priority to spend more time with them. Carson and Bob could criticize me every day for not doing enough in this area, but that criticism isn't likely to motivate me to work harder at reaching my goals. Rather, they have committed to affirm me when they "catch me doing it right." This positive encouragement will likely bring about more progress than putting me down and making me feel miserable. If you want to help a friend make some changes in his life, why not try to do it through affirmation rather than criticism?

Stop Blaming

A number of years ago, one of our vice presidents at Dominion Construction experienced a great deal of success in turning around what had previously been a "hard luck" division. As his division began to demonstrate sustained success, I became curious about how this had been accomplished and asked him what was behind this miraculous turnaround. His answer was simple—and quite unexpected. He said, "One day, I decided to stop blaming." He went on to explain that it had previously been all too easy to blame his secretary, his clients, his staff, or even his superiors if things weren't going the way he wanted. Since he had chosen to take responsibility and to abandon blaming others, he had become one of our most effective executives. In fact, his attitude had transformed his previously lackluster group into a tightly knit, successful and profitable team.

How about you? Like me, do you often fall into the trap of blaming others? In his great book *Don't Sweat the Small Stuff,* psychologist Dr. Richard Carlson provides the following observations about blame: "We typically think that if something is missing, someone else must have moved it; or if your expenses exceed your income, then your spouse must be spending too much money. Or if the house is a mess, you must be the only person doing your part."[7] The list of complaints and blame assessing could go on.

Instead, Carlson says, "When the house is a mess, clean it up! When you're over budget, figure out where you can spend less money." He also adds, "Blaming others takes an enormous amount of mental energy. It's a 'drag me down' mind-set that creates stress."

Since reading this, I have worked at avoiding blaming in every area of my life, particularly when speaking with Carson and Bob. They aren't blamers, but when we're talking about the challenges we face in life, it would be easy to slip into a pattern of blaming. Instead of placing blaming on others, taking responsibility for what is going on in our lives provides us with a more proactive approach and thus offers us the opportunity to make a positive change that will influence events, not just respond to them.[8] We affirm one another as we take responsibility, and that motivates us to make the changes that will bring about success—just as our company's vice president did.

Conclusion

Do you remember when I wrote down my thirteen weaknesses and asked Bob to help me improve in these areas? Well, the truth is, I didn't need Bob to remind me of them; I knew them all too well. And I didn't need Bob to criticize me for my weaknesses; I already had enough criticism in my life. What I needed was affirmation that would encourage me as I faced the day-to-day challenges of life and motivate me to make the changes that would help diminish my weaknesses and faults. My soul brothers have promised to encourage me to become the best that I can be.

Who affirms you? Whom can you affirm? Why not take some time now to think about it?

Out of the same mouth came praise and cursing. . . .
This should not be.

—James 3:10, NIV

Let us consider how we may spur one another on toward love and good deeds. . . . Let us encourage one another.

—Hebrews 10:24, 25, NIV

Chapter 5

Who Has Time for Friends Anyway?

Covenant of Availability: I will make time, energy, insight, and possessions freely available when needed and in proper relationship to my other covenant commitments. As part of this availability, I pledge my time on a regular basis, whether in prayer or in an agreed upon meeting time.

"How's it going?"
"Busy.... You?"
"Man, I'm really busy! It's crazy around here!"

Sound familiar? It's a typical exchange when two people pass each other during the day. But here's a challenge—the next time someone asks how you are, why not respond with something other than "busy."

One summer while taking a sabbatical, I had a rare commodity on my hands—free time. I didn't have to punch a clock, didn't have to be at the office, and didn't have an endless to-do list. And yet, I found that I was always looking for ways to keep busy. After all, every successful person wants to *look* and *feel* busy—it's part of our North American culture. We somehow feel more important if we are busy; and feel guilty if we aren't.

In the midst of our perpetually overcrowded schedules, few of us are able to make time for the things we really want to do or for the friends with whom we really want to spend time. Knowing this reality, Carson, Bob, and I have promised in our covenant that we will not let busyness keep us from being available to each other. To be honest, we too often fail in this area, but we are dedicated to continuing to bring our actions in line with our intentions. The covenant is our reminder.

Learning to Just "Be" Together

American author and pastor, Stu Weber, writes, "Most of us think we have to conjure up 'practical' reasons or excuses for picking up the phone and calling another man."[1] Indeed, as I mentioned in chapter 2, many men make the assumption that an agenda is—or must be—present for any interaction to occur. In contrast, Dr. Richard Halverson, a well-known devotional writer and former chaplain to the U.S. Senate, states that our agendas should spring from our encounters and the needs of the people we are with—including our own. He points to Jesus of Nazareth as a model for this behavior:

> Personally, I've always been amazed by the story of when Jesus encountered a blind man who had come to him to be healed. Obviously, being God, Jesus knew what the man wanted and obviously, having the capacity to heal him, I am sure he knew why the man had come to him. However, rather than just diving on in and healing him, Jesus began the encounter by saying, "What do you want me to do for you?" So often we want to get on with our agendas, and we assume we know what others want.[2]

Dr. Halverson concludes that "being with each other is an end in itself."[3] But I'm convinced that before we can get to this place in our expectations and relationships, we need to experience a paradigm shift in our hearts—and that requires that we invest in, or maybe even squander, time just being together.

For those of us who are task-oriented, being available and just "being" with someone can be hard work. It requires a clear resolve to build the fabric of friendship with no strings attached. Perhaps we could begin by grabbing our calendars or palm pilots and block out specific times to be with our friends, well in advance. This would shield our friendships from the pressures of urgent activities or lesser commitments. For example, if you think about the time you spend watching television or movies, surfing the Web, or nursing a cup of coffee or a beer, you might realize, that you have more discretionary time available than you thought, time that could be recaptured for building friendships.

In a sense, the very invitation to "get together for a beer" may be pointing toward this idea of "just being together." When we say, "Let's go for a beer, or a coffee," the real invitation often represents a desire to interact without an agenda present.

If you have experienced falling in love, you know about the feelings of wanting to "be together"—not to do anything in particular, just to be together. I've been told that most dating couples spend sixteen hours a week together. However, once married and the honeymoon ended, they are too busy to give each other one hour a week. Similarly, if we really want to invest in friendship, the time is there; we just have to determine to start. As Mark Twain quipped, "The secret of getting ahead is getting started." In other words, the best starting point for friendship may simply be scheduling it into your agenda.

In our covenant, we have resolved not to let our schedules or our natural task orientation keep us from learning the skill to simply be together for no particular purpose. We each still have some learning to do in this area. In the summer of 1999, my family spent some holiday time with Bob's family and, later, onboard our family boat with Carson's family. But as time drew us closer to each vacation, I recall wondering what "things" we should "do," and what we should determine to "accomplish" while together. Were there topics we needed to discuss or projects we needed to advance?

It helped me to remember that part of our covenant is simply a commitment to spending time together. Looking back now, I realize that these days produced some of our happiest times together as families. It was a new experience for me to just *"be,"* without having to accomplish something. I must confess that I still had a list of activities such as skiing, hiking, visiting, and sailing that I tried to squeeze into our days. But, activity lists aside, I finally felt free to judge our time worthwhile regardless of whether or not we did any of these things.

Setting Aside the Need to Fix Things

Sometimes "being there" is accomplished by spending time together, but on other occasions, "being" there can simply mean being quiet—listening and not trying to "fix" things.

One day, Carson admitted to me that he felt like a failure in several of his roles. I pressed him for more discussion, but he said he really didn't want to talk about it. As his friend, I was frustrated. I am task-oriented by nature. Generally I like to deal with problems the same way I deal with my other tasks—by preparing a list of goals, tackling them one by one, and putting a tick beside each item as it is accomplished. As a result, I was anxious to fix things for Carson. That was when Carson rocked me back on my heels by uttering the true cry of his heart, "I don't want you to try to fix things! I just want you to be here, to be with me and to support me."

As I consider this situation now, I realize that I would have done well to recall the biblical story of Job, a godly man who was considered blameless, yet suffered through devastating losses and trials. When his friends heard about his troubles, "they set out from their homes and met together by agreement to go and sympathize with him and comfort him;. . . they sat on the ground with him for seven days and seven nights. No one said a word to him, because they saw how great his suffering was" (Job 2:11, 13).

Being silently present beside a suffering friend is an extraordinary expression of compassion and solidarity. It is a great compliment to give to a friend in pain, and is often of greater value than any words of wisdom that we might have to offer. After all, it is when Job's friends broke their silence to speak their advice and speculate about why they thought he was suffering that they brought discouragement to him. Instead of advice, Job needed their understanding and encouragement.

Men are often quick to pass out advice; it is their nature. But Dr. Larry Crabb says, "We will not heal many souls when advice or instruction is at the center of our efforts. Our power to influence lives does not come from telling people what to do. Nor does it come from revealing to people the details of their inner mess."[4] Rather, there are times when "men need to hold back on giving advice . . . and just be patient."[5] It is a difficult lesson for busy people with busy schedules to comprehend. As for me, I am slowly making progress. I am learning that savoring time in the company of another can be a great reward in and of itself.

Seven Steps to Finding Time for Friends

You will likely encounter some difficulties and frustration as you begin to reshape your schedule to include time to cultivate friendships. Here are seven concepts that may give you patience as you consider ways to make practical changes in your daily schedule.

1. *Commitment.* As in everything, a clear resolve is necessary for achievement. If you want to find time to be together with friends, the first step is to simply decide. If you are going to make these relationships a priority, start by making a commitment to invest in friendship.

2. *Perspective.* Take time to get off the treadmill periodically to gain some perspective. My dad *never* worked on Sunday, and this day of rest and reflection gave a certain rhythm to his life. Bob goes out on an overnight retreat at least four times a year just to review his priorities and "recalibrate." Bob, Carson, and I now try to do this together, realizing that the physical change in routine along with the input of others will better enable us to see our lives in a true light.

3. *Planning.* Schedule friendship time in your calendar *first.* If we wait to fit our friends into the "leftover" spaces, we will likely never establish anything other than marginal friendships.

4. *Shift your paradigm.* U.S. President Jimmy Carter took the time every week to teach Sunday school during his four-year term in the White House. If one of the busiest executives in the world can find time for this personal priority, then surely we can make time for the things that matter most to us.

5. *Be humble.* If you think your company, your clients, your industry, or your ministry cannot survive without you, your ego is likely clouding your judgment. What many of us mistakenly think of as duty is too often an overinflated sense of our own self-importance. The world will still keep turning if we stop for a couple of hours each week to spend time with a friend. In truth, the world would likely be a better place if we all took this advice to heart.

6. *Choose to live with margin.* This is an area of real challenge for me, as I don't like to waste time. I see life as a precious gift and each moment as an opportunity. Lately, I'm realizing that I

should abandon my belief that more is more and learn instead to do less . . . better. This in turn will give me not just time, but also energy for the relationships that matter.

7. *Listen and learn.* Our spouses can often assist us to re-order our lives to accommodate friendship. As those closest to us, they know the pressures of our schedules, yet also understand the need we have to invest in friendship. As a result, they could assist us to make time for what really matters.

Conclusion

Today, life's pace is increasingly hectic. While e-mail, cell phones, and P.D.A.'s enable us to accomplish more tasks, they also bring with them the expectation that we should be doing even more within that same period of time. As our expectations continue to exceed the number of hours available to us each day, we have to make increasingly more difficult choices about where we invest our time. It seems that there will always be something worthwhile, profitable, or seemingly urgent that must be done. Constantly choosing work or other activities will cause friendship to always be relegated to the margins of our lives.

Remember chapter 1? Transformational friendship is radically different. By choosing to invest time in friendship we are doing something that is out of the norm, against the current of contemporary life. Quality friendship can be a goal that you actively strive toward, just as you would endeavor to achieve success in your career or a sporting activity. Being proactive about putting friendship on our agendas first, and then scheduling other activities around it, is radical and different. But the dividends are fantastic.

Though one may be overpowered, two can defend themselves. A cord of three strands is not quickly broken.

—Ecclesiastes 4:12, NIV

Chapter 6

Whom Can You Call during a Crisis?

Covenant of Prayer: I covenant to regularly pray for you, believing that our caring Father wishes his children to pray for one another and ask him for the blessings they need and the desires of their hearts.

I hope that as you read this book you are getting a glimpse of God's presence and significance in our lives. Gordon MacDonald writes, "Friendships may be the key building blocks of your spiritual life."[1] This statement has proven true in our covenant friendship where we view friendship with God and with each other as complementary pursuits. That is, as our friendship spurs us on in our relationship with God, it encourages our growth in the spiritual realm. In turn, we each develop a greater capacity to properly love and influence our friends. This is the transforming power of friendship at its best.

In our covenant, Bob, Carson, and I have promised to pray for each other. By being purposeful about praying together, we help each other to reach out to God. By being purposeful about praying for each other, we cry out to God on each other's behalf. As you will see, our friendship has been made far more influential and supportive as a result.

Is God Listening?

It is said that there are no atheists in foxholes. That is, if and when we are faced with impending death, most of us cry out to God for help in the hopes that he is listening. . . . Even the most hardened of hearts can be caught entreating God when misfortune or panic grips them. You may not call it prayer, but when you have reached the end of your own resources, I would presume that you've called out—even in alarm or frustration—for God or for somebody, somewhere to come to your aid.

As irreverent as some of our language may be when we call on God, I believe that we all subconsciously acknowledge his existence by doing so. And, in most cases, our cry is an expression of hope that he is there.

Why Some Men Don't Pray

Some men may not want to pray simply because intimacy with God is a foreign concept and, therefore, rather frightening. Few of us relish the opportunity to delve into the mystical side of things. Or perhaps we fear that if we've had a friendship with God, it might influence and, ultimately, change our lives. Instead, we would prefer to remain in control, living the life that we want and are familiar with.

In *Seeking the Face of God*, Gary Thomas accurately sums up this fear: "We are spiritually fearful people, and alone before God, we stand naked and vulnerable. We won't be able to pretend anymore. . . . We will have the choice to obey or disobey, but pretending will no longer be an option."[2]

For others, it's less complicated. Perhaps a poor relationship with an earthly father has made us afraid of what a heavenly father might be like. Others may simply not be in the habit of praying or can't find the time to pray. Perhaps we think of ourselves as not "spiritual" enough. This was a real issue for me, and my friends have helped me to develop a more regular pattern of prayer and interacting with God (as discussed later, in chapter 17).

Regardless of our reasons, we may draw back from God in the same way we recoil from interactions with a dentist or a doctor. We fear that they might want to pull a tooth, or tamper with some part or another, even though we know that it is necessary to reestablish our good health. Consequently, we often elect to carry on with our maladies and deny ourselves good health if it means we can avoid the temporary pain of the drill or the needle.

But God is nearer than we think. We only need to open our hearts and minds to God's presence to engage in communication with him. My friends have helped me to learn more about prayer and have helped me to become comfortable about praying at times other than meals or in a church. Learning to pray requires perseverance, especially if our prayers seem not to be answered, simply bouncing off the ceiling. But if we keep at it, we will be heard and, most importantly, we will develop the confidence that we are being heard.

Prayers for Work

Perhaps you've experienced that gut-wrenching knot of fear when confronted with major issues at work. We wake up to the reality that we have little control over what is happening, and it's at that moment that we have a choice. Do we call out to God? Or do we feel obligated to face life on our own?

I can vividly recall several occasions where I felt almost paralyzed with fear and the prayers of a friend were extremely helpful. In one such case, prayer gave me peace as I related to my uncle, the CEO of our family company. Although Bob and I had enjoyed a promising beginning to our working relationship, it eventually deteriorated badly. I need to shoulder much of the blame for this, because in my iconoclastic and impatient style, I had been openly critical of him and had poisoned our relationship. (I am very sorry that I didn't show him the respect that he was due and have since apologized to him for this.) However, one day I received a summons to his office. We hadn't been working together for some time, and I was puzzled by his request to meet. To be frank, I was terrified. I had no idea what lay ahead, but because of our strained relationship, I feared the worst.

I called Carson on my cell phone as I walked between the five office towers that bear my family's name and comprise the Bentall Centre in downtown Vancouver. I sat down on a granite bench in the plaza between buildings and literally trembled as Carson prayed on my behalf. Connected by the wonders of technology, we placed my concerns before God. It's hard to describe the sense of relief, confidence, and renewed faith I felt having had that brief interlude of prayer with a friend. My fears did not all disappear, but I was a calmer, gentler person as I entered my uncle's office. To be honest, today I can hardly even remember what he wanted to talk to me about. I think it related to a property transaction, and he simply wanted to have my recollection of the deal. In other words, it was nothing that I really needed to be afraid of.

Most of us can probably remember at least some of the Ten Commandments. Don't murder; don't steal. But what about the commandment found in Philippians 4:6—"Don't worry about anything." The next verse offers the promise that if we pray, God will "give us peace."

In my relationships with Carson and Bob, it has been remarkable how we have been able to reach out to God when times have been hard and pray together. "The peace that passes all understanding" (Philippians 4:7) has consistently been the reward for our prayers, just like it was the day I met with my uncle.

Prayers for Marriage

Alison and I have been married for more than twenty-five years now and, like any couple, we have had our ups and downs. On more than one occasion, I have reached out for the support and advice of my prayer partners, sometimes with tears staining my cheeks or while sitting in my car, unable to "go on." It has been these prayers "over the wire" that have enabled me to gain perspective and strength to continue on in my relationship with Alison.

As a group, the three of us have committed to encourage each other in our spiritual walk and to stimulate each other toward greater intimacy with God. This doesn't need to be "formal," because prayer can be as natural as the conversations we engage in with our friends. This means that we will pray for each other and encourage each other at all times—not just in the "foxholes of life."

Prayers for Our Children

According to Carson, our prayers with each other—and for each other—are the greatest benefit of our covenant friendship. He describes prayer as taking an inward journey together—an adventure where the three of us can gather, knowing that nothing can separate us from the love of God or from the love of each other. As a result of this spiritual freedom, we have had a number of meaningful and memorable experiences through prayer. Carson relates one experience when prayer helped to transform me and my relationship with my daughter:

> *Carson:* One evening, David began to tell us about his relationship with Christy and how frustrated he was with some of their more recent interactions. Being the typical father, he had been trying to influence her goals with regard to school, career, friends, finances, etc. Being the typical young adult, Christy had her own ideas about what her priorities should be.
>
> Before I continue, let me say that I feel very much like "Uncle Carson" to Christy. She is a grown woman now, but every time I see her, my heart almost melts as I recall my earliest memories of her as a tiny baby. Christy suffered from colic, and my wife Brenda and I would frequently go over to give Dave and Alison a break from Christy's constant crying. We would take this little bundle in our arms and cradle her for hours until she would fall asleep—more from exhaustion than anything else. I prayed for Christy during those long hours; I prayed regularly for her as she grew older; and I still pray for her today as she approaches her university graduation. So the bottom line is—don't mess with my Christy! By being committed to her dad, I am committed to her and will pray for her always! In fact, my own sons continue to tease me about my affection for Christy by reminding me that I once gave her my credit card when she wanted to go out. It was an experience that I certainly hadn't given them! But back to the subject at hand.
>
> After David explained what had been happening with them over the preceding months, I asked him whether he felt his behavior was helping or hindering Christy to develop her life as independent adult. We looked at some Scripture passages together to help bring a "higher" perspective to the situation and to change the focus of the discussion. Later on, the three of us bowed our heads and prayed together for both Christy and David. We prayed that God would give David the courage

to release Christy into God's care and to love her with no strings attached.

As a result of these prayers and David's willingness to use some new approaches with his daughter, there is a much better understanding between them. They now report that they have opened a new and positive chapter in their father-daughter relationship.

Conclusion

There are no rules for prayer, nor any proper time to pray, nor precise words to use. When the friendship is trusting and focused on calling out the very best that God has put into each person, the words will usually come to us. Somehow, through our imperfect prayers together, God transforms us. And, somehow, when we pray for each other, God gives us strength and enables us to "stumble heavenward" together.

And when you come before God, don't turn that into a theatrical production. . . . All these people making a regular show out of their prayers, hoping for stardom! Do you think God sits in a box seat?

Here's what I want you to do; find a quiet secluded place so you won't be tempted to role-play before God. . . .

This is your Father you are dealing with . . . . You can pray very simply.

Matthew 6:5, 6, 9b, *The Message*

Chapter 7

Why Should I Share My Weaknesses with You?

Covenant of Openness: I promise to strive to become a more open, vulnerable person, disclosing my hurts to you. I desire to trust you with my problems and my dreams. This is to affirm your worth to me as a person.

There I was, sitting in a circle with fifty other successful business executives, feeling very much as though I was back in grade one but determined to make the most of it. Each of us was then asked to describe ourselves to the others using just three words. After some careful thought, I chose the words *faith, integrity,* and *transparency.* The group seemed to accept the first two as appropriate descriptions, but there were more than a few puzzled looks from my colleagues when I mentioned the third. It *was* an unusual choice, I admit. But nothing prepared me for the reaction it received.

It seemed that transparency was such a foreign notion to these men that they thought I must have been mistaken in my thinking. When the session was over, several approached me to say, "You didn't really mean to use that word, did you?" Some of them thought I was referring to myself as invisible! The dictionary defines *transparent* as "open, frank, or candid" and I certainly want to be like this, so yes, I really meant to use *transparent.*

When I am with my covenant partners, my transparency enables me to share openly and candidly about my life, even when I'm not trying to. The other guys joke, "You always know what's going on with David," because I don't hide my feelings very easily. In fact, it's probably a good thing that I never play poker. But beyond all this, I know that my transparency is a gift that I bring to our group. My emotions and my heart are available to them without their having to probe excessively or to dig to get beneath the surface. In other words, with me, you might say that what you see is what you get.

Transparency Can Build Relationships

I first learned about the importance of transparency as it relates to friendship from Dr. James (Jim) Houston. This author and professor, who taught for many years at Oxford, once told me that "friendship is built on the mutual sharing of weakness." I considered it an interesting concept but, at the time, I was convinced that friendship was rooted more in common interests than in being transparent with others—especially if it meant sharing weaknesses.

I was thinking about this idea a short time later, while traveling. On the plane, I was seated next to an acquaintance who was a dynamic and creative entrepreneur. As we talked, I told him about Jim's theory on the mutual sharing of weakness and admitted that it just didn't make sense to me. As the conversation continued, I confessed that I didn't think he and I could ever be close friends because he was far too intelligent and I felt intimidated. To my amazement, he reciprocated by explaining that he didn't think we could ever be friends either. He felt uncomfortable and insecure because I came from a wealthy family. In short, we were convinced friendship was out of our reach—I thought he was too smart and he thought I was too rich!

You can probably guess what happened. As a result of this mutual sharing of our feelings of inadequacy, a friendship began to form. Dr. Houston's theory had proved to be true, even as we discussed why we thought it false. In the twenty years since then, I have discovered time and again that if you share something of yourself, including some weakness or inadequacy, others will almost invariably warm to you or reciprocate by sharing their own weaknesses.

Motivational speaker and life coach Dr. Ron Jenson writes about similar experiences when sharing weaknesses:

Often when I speak publicly, I talk about some weakness in my life. I have plenty of illustrations, and I'm glad to share them. The response is never, "Oh, Jenson, you're worse than I thought!" Instead, people say, "Oh, and thank you. I'm so glad to know someone else is struggling in an area where I've struggled." People don't respect me less, they respect me all the more because I admit my weaknesses.[1]

We often lose out on such positive experiences and opportunities to bond with one another because our ingrained, competitive attitudes naturally encourage us to play from our strengths and not our weaknesses.

Using Discretion to Govern What We Publicly Share

The good news is that we can easily encourage others to be more open by speaking about ourselves with honesty and *without* the usual pretense. As we do, others are often more willing to enter that same level of intimacy. I recall once being interviewed as part of a three-person panel of family business owners at a two-hundred-guest gala dinner. We were each asked to communicate about our experiences working in a family business. The other two panelists seemed quite hesitant to speak initially, perhaps not wanting to reveal too much information. However, as they observed me quite freely sharing my experiences, good and bad, they too began to be more transparent. They opened up about what their experiences had been in their family corporations, all to the benefit of our audience.

I am not advocating a compulsive airing of dirty laundry. In the above situation, none of us disclosed information to the audience that was in any way inappropriate. We still showed discretion in our words. But discretion and transparency don't have to be mutually exclusive. In most cases, with a little forethought, we can determine what is or isn't appropriate to share. This varies with the situation.

Most of us don't like to tell our most intimate secrets or experiences to anyone but close friends, with whom there is a preexisting bond of trust. Furthermore, our most intimate life experiences and friendships will only remain meaningful or significant if we show discretion in what we share and with whom we share. In short, by advocating that we shed our pretenses and our public persona when we meet people, I am not suggesting indiscriminating self-disclosure. Rather, I am encouraging an appropriate transparency that can be a big step to creating an open and sharing friendship.

Using Discretion to Govern What We Privately Share

Being transparent requires a safe environment in which to share our fears and struggles. A safe place to discuss will help us endeavor to overcome them. That is most appropriately done within the context of an ongoing relationship.

Growing in our ability to be transparent with friends, however, doesn't give us a license to speak to them about others in a negative or hurtful way. As a family, we used to have these words posted on our refrigerator: "Is it true, is it kind, is it necessary?" I'm sure that many of us would have much less to say if we took the time to ask these three questions before saying any thing, to any one.

For example, if I'm having a difficult time getting along with another person, it may be appropriate to ask one of my covenant partners for a suggestion that would enable me to improve that relationship. However, to expose all the details of someone else's injury to me or to focus the discussion on his or her inadequacies (in the name of openness or transparency or even in request for prayer) is a travesty. Instead, my transparency should be focused on how I am responding to the issue or on what's happening within me—not on what others are thinking, saying, or doing—or not doing.

There are two benefits that result when I keep the discussion focused on me: first, I avoid spreading negativism or criticism or gossip and, second, I am not focusing on changing others. I can only change myself. If I can discipline myself to avoid blaming and judging others and face my own inadequacies, it is like adding fertilizer and sunshine to a crop; I begin to grow.

Using Discretion to Govern Our Expectations of Others

Discretion is widely considered to be an old-fashioned concept that died years ago. Think about current attitudes toward sexual freedom and how many people are comfortable with baring it all on a first date. In such cases, it is self-evident that the more casual we are with sharing our bodies in sexual intimacy, the less meaningful or significant the act becomes. Similarly, with regard to vulnerability in friendship, we are wise to use discretion to avoid verbally baring all without first building a bond of trust and caring. It isn't always appropriate to divulge intimate struggles nor to expect that others will share their deepest feelings.

I must admit that sometimes I am transparent to a fault. Being open and vulnerable can be an endearing trait, but when taken to an extreme it can prove to be both unwise and intimidating to others. I recall a time when guests had gathered at my family's home to sing carols and celebrate the Christmas season. As I spoke with one young woman, it became apparent that she was quite discouraged. I pressed her to tell more about her struggles. I truly wanted to understand and to offer my help or support. Unfortunately, my encouraging her to elaborate only resulted in offending her—she felt that I was trivializing her issues by trying to talk about them over hors d'oeuvres at a Christmas party.

I learned an important lesson that night. We can't just dip in and out of people's lives when seeking intimacy. Doing so promotes a sort of "relational strip-tease,"[2] that is, it pushes others to shed their dignity while simultaneously diminishing our own sense of integrity. In this particular case, there was no previous bond of trust or commitment between us and, as I have since learned, the woman was wise to recoil. In part, she may have been responding to what she perceived as a man who was overly interested in her life. I hadn't earned the right to know her deepest concerns.

This point was illustrated in an episode of the popular TV series *Seinfeld.* The "show about nothing" featured a discussion about how unappealing it is to take off your clothes in the presence of others. Being seen naked was compared to the embarrassment one might experience if caught, unaware, going to the toilet in public. Certainly, most of us would be mortified at the thought of "dropping our drawers in the mall." Similarly, we may fear similar embarrassment when considering the kind of self-disclosure that may be necessary to establish candor in friendship. But, a certain amount of risk is requisite in friendship, as in any situation where there's a possibility of rejection or loss.

Transparency and a Major Career Decision

At one point in my career I was contemplating whether to buy or sell a major interest in our family business, Dominion Construction. I was the only member of the family still actively working in the company and held the positions of president and CEO. I also owned 40 percent of the company shares, with two sisters sharing the balance of the ownership. They encouraged me to make an offer to purchase their shares so they could simplify their estate planning. (I am considerably younger than my sisters.) This would also enable me to consolidate ownership of the company in our branch of the family. I was somewhat hesitant, because I wasn't convinced that I wanted to spend the rest of my life in the construction industry. Ultimately, however, I made what I believed to be a fair offer.

My proposal was deemed to be a little lower than expected, and so, in accordance with our co-owners agreement, one sister countered my offer. This was all done in a friendly but delicate manner. Under the terms of our shareholders' agreement, I had ample time to consider the offer, accept it, or counter at a higher price.

Considering my twenty-year personal involvement with the business, it was a gut-wrenching decision that was not based on economics alone. The company was highly successful and was well known across North America. If I were to sell my shares, I would almost certainly be discontinuing any involvement with the business enterprise that had been so successfully managed by both my father and my grandfather before him. In a way, I would be turning my back on my family's heritage.

Carson, Bob, and I happened to go on a retreat at the time I was wrestling with this decision. I discussed the options with them. When Bob asked me at some point what I would do if I had the opportunity to buy another construction company, I explained that I wouldn't be interested. It was only our family's previous involvement and a sense of stewardship that attracted me to Dominion, not a love for the construction industry itself.

As I offered this reply, I realized that I had found the key to my decision. I blurted out to Bob, "You know what? If I owned another construction company, I wouldn't hire me to run it either." When asked why, I explained, "I'm not passionate about construction and I think you need to have passion to do well in any endeavor." Once I had uttered those words, the decision became self-evident; I should accept my sister's offer and sell my interest in the company.

Given our family's prominence in the business community, I would not have been able to discuss this situation with Carson and Bob unless I was absolutely certain it would be treated with confidentiality. Moreover, I probably wouldn't have shared it with them if I had thought that they would try to push me into a decision. It was their supportive, caring friendship that enabled me to share what I was really thinking and to give them the insight to question how my true passions related to my career.

Conclusion

Despite the benefits to transparency, it is a fact that many men are willing to share difficulties and struggles only when they are past. If we failed at something in elementary school, we can look back at it, talk about it, and even laugh at ourselves. Yet somehow we tend to keep our current difficulties secret, even though these are the only problems with which our friends can help.

In our culture, boys learn early that "big boys don't cry." This male socialization is reinforced throughout high school and university, as men are subtly and not so subtly encouraged to be self-reliant. I've been there, so I realize that it requires quite a reverse of assumptions and thought processes to be able to openly share struggles with our friends. But, if we can learn to be open and vulnerable with a few trusted friends, a major obstacle to the path to meaningful friendship will have been successfully navigated. After all, the open sharing of struggles gives friends the opportunity to walk alongside us, to listen, to counsel, or to simply provide companionship.

Take a moment to consider the words *friend* and *ship.* Friendship is essentially a state of being in the same boat, or ship, as someone else. Fellow vacationers taking a cruise to Alaska share a destination in common, placing their safety and security in a common vessel. In the same way, through friendship, men can choose to create a common environment where they can openly share struggles with each other. As a result, we can shield one another from the storms of life and give each other encouragement and advice on how to handle the bad—and good—weather. Contrary to societal conditioning, we men don't have to be alone on the bridge, piloting our lives without any support when the sea gets rough. We can have other hands on deck when we need them.

Bear one another's burdens and so fulfill the law of love.

—Galatians 6:2

Chapter 8

Can You Trust Others to Tell You the Truth?

Covenant of Honesty: I will try to mirror back to you to what I am hearing you say. If this means risking pain for either of us, I will trust our mutual covenant enough to take that risk, realizing it is in "speaking the truth in love that we grow up in every way into Christ who is the head" (Ephesians 4:15). I will try to express this honestly in a sensitive and controlled manner and to monitor it according to what I perceive your needs to be.

Honesty is an increasingly rare quality. I therefore feel privileged to be a member of a covenant that is committed to honesty and to creating a sphere of relationships where the truth is both honored and preserved.

Ironically, being truthful can become more difficult as we get to know one another. We begin to see each other's weaknesses more clearly, faults become more noticeable, and some faults continue to surface week after week. It is tempting to give in to frustration and judgment. We may even want to use "truth" as a license to shoot one another down—particularly when we observe a prolonged inability to conquer certain shortcomings. Conversations can easily become focused on criticism. We may want to tell our friends exactly what they need to do in order to get their act together. We then find ourselves saying, "Why can't you?" or "You should."

Dr. Ron Jenson is an internationally known speaker and executive consultant who is also widely known as "America's Life Coach." He encourages men to be honest but not judgmental as we attempt to influence one another. We don't need to abandon our critical thinking skills, but we do need to monitor our attitude as we express our honest thoughts.[1] That's why, in our covenant, we seek to mirror, rather than judge, what we hear or see in each other's lives. We try to explain what we see, and then we ask if our observations ring true. If we are mirroring to each other effectively, our discussions will be characterized more by curiosity than criticism, as we use words such as "I'm wondering if you are aware" or "Have you noticed?" In doing so, we are able to clarify our thoughts, while steering clear of judgmental attitudes.

Some people believe in being brutally honest. That is, if you are a "real man" it is assumed that you should be able to take the truth and face it head on. This may be true for some, but it is often unnecessary and sometimes unwise. Frankly, there is nothing that can be said with brutal honesty that can't be said better with some degree of sensitivity. If your goal is to help others grow and change, you may need to be direct. But brutal, insensitive honesty tends to raise the defenses of the person on the receiving end and often ends up hurting more than it helps.

Friends Are Committed to Honesty

Carson is the president of Arrow Leadership Ministries, and for several years I acted as chairman of the board. Bob had been the previous chair, and when I took on the role, it was at the request of both Carson and Bob. I was somewhat reluctant, because I was concerned that at times this role might create circumstances that could bring disagreement or disharmony to my friendship with Carson.

Sure enough, last year it became clear to me that Carson and I differed in our preferences as to how certain things should be done. As his friend, I considered carefully how to approach this situation. I wanted to be honest, but I also wanted to preserve our friendship.

In such situations there is often a temptation to tell a white lie that, we rationalize, will pose no risk to the relationship. I could have said, "Carson, I'm getting too busy to continue as the board chair," then quietly withdrew as chair, without any fuss. But the problem with that was simple—it wouldn't be the truth.

Rather than lie, I decided honestly and without judgment to communicate my concerns to Carson. One afternoon, while we were on retreat at Westminster Abbey in Mission, British Columbia, Carson and I went for a walk together. We talked about a wide range of subjects before the opportunity to discuss this relatively delicate matter presented itself. I started off by asking Carson to tell me about his experiences and observations with positive board-management relationships. I was not surprised to learn that he had experienced few, if any, such positive relationships. With this as a backdrop, I explained that I thought it was unlikely that we could build a great board-chair relationship, pointing out two key problems. First, Carson's experiences had given him few positive role models regarding board-staff relations. Second, Carson saw me as a peer and had difficulty seeing me as his supervisor, which I would need to be as board chairman.

I explained this honestly and then suggested that I was willing to step aside and let Carson find a chair more compatible with him. Alternatively, I stated I was willing to stay on the board, with the condition that we develop a different kind of chair-president relationship. After reflecting on this discussion for a few weeks, Carson concluded he would like to find a new chair. I remained until he could find a replacement for me. We have both been very pleased with the results since.

Did we handle this in an exemplary way? I don't know. One board member, however, was very affirming of the process. In fact, he remarked that he was amazed at how we were able to keep our friendship as a priority as we worked through this difficult issue.

The challenge in such situations is to communicate honestly, yet in a way that avoids undermining the relationship. Our covenant provides the promise that our support for one another will not be withdrawn if we disagree. This is not a license for careless, unthinking interaction. In *Sacred Companions,* David Benner writes:

> Honesty is not just something that friends try to practice. It is also something they delight in experiencing. The honesty that characterizes genuine and deep friendship is not just the honesty of words. It is also the honesty of being. Friends feel

sufficiently safe with each other that they can relax and be what they are. Since I am already known and loved for who I am, pretensions can be set aside and I can be myself.[2]

Carson and I have a deeper relationship as a result of this encounter. Why? In part, because we know more about each other, but also because we have chosen to risk misunderstanding in order to honor one another.

Be Honest with Me

Carson: I once faced an accusation that had the potential of ending my ministerial career. David and Bob were instrumental in holding me up during what seemed like an impossible situation. Bob was switching back and forth between being my friend and my lawyer—a tricky balancing act that he exercised with integrity. He counseled me wisely, encouraging me to take a position of grace and to walk through whatever was necessary to overcome this challenge.

As part of the process, I volunteered to take a lie detector test. I realize that this isn't something that many of you will ever willingly subject yourselves to—but since then I have often thought that it might not be a bad idea if we all submitted to a periodic examination of what is in our hearts and minds.

Not to keep you in suspense any further, I passed the lie detector test and felt that honesty prevailed in the situation. In retrospect, I now believe that I came out the other side a much better person. In fact, walking through this ordeal has proven to be so foundational to my growth and development that, even though painful at the time, I would actually choose to do it again—just to reap the positive changes that it brought about.

Through it all, Bob and I experienced a new level of honesty in our friendship that has only deepened our love for each another. Since then, we have each gone through significant challenges that have continued to increase our respect, and our desire, for honesty in relationships. Once you experience an authentic, honest relationship—all others smack of superficiality. I think that each of us needs a friend who is close enough to look us right in the eyes and say, "BS," when appropriate.

Could I have gone through this alone? I don't think so. Daniel Goleman writes that three or more situations of intense stress within one year triple the death rate in socially isolated, middle-aged men.[3] But stress events have no impact whatsoever on the death rate of men who cultivate close relationships!

On a lighter note, honesty at this level guarantees a long-standing relationship. Over time, you have enough "dirt" on each other that you have to remain friends for life (written with a smile).

Superficiality Is a Barrier to Honesty

It's easier to have relationships that don't wrestle with issues of substance if we hide our problems. After all, our closest friends need never know about the difficult issues that inevitably occur in all our lives. At the office, we talk about the weather, the stock market, or who's going to win the playoffs. We all know that life is more than raindrops, bank accounts, and championships—yet even friends struggle to get past this basic level of communication.

In part, this difficulty is a matter of habit. We have come to expect, "How are you?" to always be followed by, "Fine," and so the pattern is quickly established. Conversations of depth rarely fit in. The truth is that it takes time to communicate more personally, and we each have a fear that if we ask a friend how things really are, we may get more than we bargained for or more than we know how to handle. After all, going below the surface can get messy.

I know a couple that had been married for many years and seemed to have a perfect relationship. They seemed happy when together and led a prosperous and successful life. Yet, years later, as their marriage crumbled, they confessed that they "hardly knew each other." Apparently, they related well at superficial levels but had never learned to honestly share with each other or with their friends. What a tragedy. Unfortunately, this scenario is not uncommon in marriage, or in friendship. Like ships in the night, we pass one another never really knowing each other. We settle for superficiality rather than risking honesty.

Unfortunately, we will not be able to help and encourage one another if we suppress or ignore the existence of unpleasant, difficult issues. Our friendship covenant is a promise to each other that our love for each isn't conditional. It enables Bob, Carson, and I to press past superficial chatter to focus on being honest with each other in a loving and supportive fashion.

Conflict Avoidance
Is a Barrier to Honesty

My dad and my grandfather were both extremely successful business executives. The virtue of character was the cornerstone upon which they built their careers. Dad was honest with clients and customers; he never withheld the truth in his business dealings and, at times, could be extremely candid in his relationships with employees. But in more personal matters, he often chose to avoid conflict and resisted addressing certain subjects if he felt they could lead to an argument. He was a believer in the conventional wisdom of seldom discussing religion and politics, knowing that these topics have been known to separate even the best of friends.

Unfortunately, his desire to avoid conflict made it difficult for him to talk honestly with his brother about future plans for the family company. For forty years, dad had worked hand in hand with this brother, Bob, to create a very substantial real estate and construction enterprise. Yet, despite sharing all these years and accomplishments, they found genuine and honest communication elusive. Tragically, their respective visions for the future of the business were in stark contrast. Dad wanted the company to remain privately owned; Bob wanted it to go public. Dad wanted to stay in both real estate and construction; Bob wanted out of construction. Dad wanted me to run the company; Bob wanted to discontinue family involvement in management. These seemingly irreconcilable differences eventually led to a convulsion in our family relationships and a painful corporate reorganization.

With the benefit of hindsight, we can see how all of this might have been avoided. Collaborative solutions could have been developed if the two brothers had been able to communicate honestly with each other earlier on.

Similarly, fear of conflict can make it difficult for friends to be honest with each other. My friend Dave Whyte, whom I mentioned earlier, taught me an early lesson about honesty. We were teenagers, and in an effort to avoid an argument that might spoil our relationship, he sent me a letter relating his concerns about a relationship I had with my (then) girlfriend. He didn't think we were right for each other but didn't want to harm his friendship with me. He cut out and pasted words from the newspaper into sentences and then sent the anonymous missive to me!

Creating mystery letters with cutout newspaper words doesn't exactly reflect maturity in dealing with honesty. But I continue to treasure this act as one of genuine kindness because it was based on two important principles of friendship. First, Dave did what all good friends should do—he observed what was going on in my life, and he determined to speak the truth to me (from his perspective). Second, he did so in a way that would preserve our friendship. The letter was a clumsy way of getting the job done, and I certainly don't advocate it as a strategy, but the act nonetheless reflects the principles of honesty and sensitivity.

Insecurity Is a Barrier to Honesty

We all want to think well of ourselves, and a healthy self-concept is necessary for normal functioning. A strong sense of ego, however, can lead people to dismiss or discount criticism, even when it's constructive, in order to preserve their own sense of self-worth. When we are blinded by our own pride, we can't be honest with ourselves or hear the honest feedback of friends. In such cases, arrogance becomes counterproductive and hinders personal growth.

Just recently, I received an e-mail message from Greg Gerrie, a former fighter pilot, and now a motivational speaker. After a friend had displayed courage in pointing out a "dramatic mistake" that Greg was making, he writes that the words weren't "easy for me to take...not at all—but he was right." Greg continued, "The lesson is this: we must not fool ourselves into thinking that we're great, that we're all-knowing, all-seeing, and all-hearing. At nearly every corner we are going to make a mistake of some kind. But our biggest mistake as a leader is the avoidance of surrounding ourselves with fellow leaders and friends who have the courage to tell us like it really is."

We can all be helped if we learn to speak the truth about ourselves to friends and then learn to listen to them as they take the risk to caringly speak truth into our world. Greg continues, "By daring to be honest with us, friends offer us invaluable opportunities for growth. They can help us penetrate our self-deceptions and cherished illusions."[4]

If we don't listen to our friend's concerns, he says, "we run the risk of losing track of who we truly and fully are and little by little come to accept instead the highly edited version which we put forth in hope that the world will find it more acceptable than the real thing.[5] "In other words, unless we learn to speak at least occasionally about who we really are, we may begin to believe our own press clippings which, sadly, don't always reflect the truth."

Conclusion

And finally, Greg says,

> It is hard to be seen at your worst. Perhaps that's why our deepest tears are often shed alone. We're afraid friends will tire of our struggles, so we keep them to ourselves, especially the ugly ones that we can't quite manage to put behind us. But tears without an audience, without someone to hear and care, leave the wounds unhealed. When someone listens to our groanings and stays there, we feel something change inside us. Despair seems less necessary; hope begins to stir where before there was only pain.[6]

Honest communication between friends isn't easy. But if we can combat the tendency to be superficial and insecure, and if we can risk the possibility of being misunderstood, disliked, or having an argument, then the relational rewards are immeasurable.

In our friendship covenant, Bob, Carson, and I are committed to telling the truth and to do so with the goal of helping each other to develop and learn. We choose to soldier on, pursuing honest communication, because we are convinced that relationships based on truth are worth preserving.

A good man is known by his truthfulness.
—Proverbs 12:17

Chapter 9

Does Anyone Really Listen to You?

Covenant of Sensitivity: Even as I desire to be known and understood by you, I covenant to be sensitive to you and to your needs to the best of my ability. I will try to hear you, see you, and feel where you are, and I will try to draw you out of discouragement or withdrawal.

Do you ever wish there was someone who would just sit back and listen to you—no matter what you have to say?

It was a late Friday afternoon in the fall of 1988, but I remember my feelings as if it were yesterday. I had been working long hours, for days on end, as president of our family company. When I turned off the lights in my office and got set to leave, I realized that I was going to miss dinner with the kids—again! It was the umpteenth time that month, and now I had let them down one more time. I had also let my wife down and, if the truth were known, I had let myself down. I didn't want life to be this way.

As I took the elevator to the ground floor of our office building and strolled across the plaza toward the parkade, I glanced up at the reflecting pool and the bust of my grandfather, the man after whom the five office towers of the Bentall Centre are named. I felt as if he was looking down at me with disappointment. He had been such a great man and always seemed to have things under control. So why couldn't I keep my life together?

All my failures began to flood my consciousness: I wasn't making the progress that I hoped for with our company, despite ten years of trying; I wasn't doing a very good job as a father, despite fifteen years of effort; I wasn't succeeding in building a happy, fulfilling marriage after almost twenty years; and I didn't feel like a very good disciple of Christ, even after thirty years. My shoulders slumped. As I shuffled toward the door of the garage, I punched Bob's number into my cell phone. He responded to my broken voice with the innocent question, "What's wrong?" Out tumbled a tirade of my seeming failures.

"I'm a failure at work, a failure at home, and a failure in everything I do!" I listed the board that I served on and lamented my inadequacy in my contribution to this group too. I then reflected on my fitness goals and how, there too, I had failed. On top of all this, I also felt the need to point out that I didn't read enough books, didn't keep up with letters to my friends, and so on. The list was endless. Bob just listened.

Once I finished, Bob remained quiet for a moment longer. Then he simply said, "You can't do everything you're trying to do. You need to give yourself some grace." At first his words didn't make sense, but as I let them sink in, they began to unshackle me. He was right. I needed to cut myself some slack. Bob could see I was overwhelmed and he responded by giving me permission to *not* have to do everything I was trying to do.

Don't get me wrong. It's important to work hard, and it's right to be committed to your family and other responsibilities. It's good to stay fit and to sharpen your mind by reading. At some point, however, we will all find ourselves failing if we try to do it all. On those occasions we can all use a friend who will come alongside us and really listen to what resides in our hearts. Bob gave me a great gift that day. In his gentle, reassuring way, he said that no matter what my accomplishments were or weren't, he still loved me—and God still loved me.

Listening with Sensitivity and Respect

As a friend, Bob has always been a great listener, and I am strengthened in knowing that he has pledged to listen to me for the rest of our lives. Years ago our friendship grew substantially as we regularly ran four or five miles together before work several times a week. Our fitness and running skills improved, but an added benefit was that as we ran, Bob patiently listened as I spilled out my difficulties, especially my confusion and stress in both my work and marriage. He heard the cry of my heart and encouraged me to press on. His caring response enabled me to get through those days.

Carson's listening skills have also been invaluable. I'll never forget the day he came over to our house just after Alison and I had experienced one of our darkest, most discouraging times together. I was upstairs in my bedroom with tears staining my cheeks. Carson came in the back door and asked Alison, on a scale of 1 to 10, how things were in our relationship. She said "minus 400!" Carson came upstairs and found me stretched out on our bed, unable to cope. He didn't try to fix things but simply said, "I'm here. What's going on?" The words were simple, but they gave me the opportunity to speak. He listened as I poured out my heart, and before long I was able to go downstairs and rejoin Alison in a spirit of forgiveness and renewal.

Bob Shares His Thoughts on Listening

Bob: Henri Nouwen writes, "The mystery of one man is too immense and too profound to be explained by another man."[1] So how can we really understand the life experiences and problems of others? Each of us is so different. That is certainly true of David and me.

I was born into humble circumstances and grew up as part of a large, extended family that shared life on a farm in the Okanagan Valley. We had little in the way of material wealth. On the other hand, David was definitely from the right side of the tracks; he was well known, well to do, and very urban. As our friendship developed, I found our differences intimidating—I didn't know that I could contribute anything to an asset-rich life, and a circumstance and life experience that I did not understand.

Ironically, it was David's father who taught me how to bridge this gulf of personal histories. Each week, Clark Bentall would invite a special guest to lunch on the thirty-second floor of Bentall Three (or occasionally at the Vancouver Club). As in-house legal counsel to the Bentall Group, I was often invited to tag along (although I sometimes felt like a street urchin being treated kindly by the rich neighbors). Clark always made a point of making me feel welcome. He often seated me beside him at the long, mahogany table beautifully set with fine silverware and china. In his kind and gentlemanly way, Clark taught me the skill of listening. He didn't just passively sit there nodding between mouthfuls. Instead, he asked probing questions that required our guests to disclose important, valuable, and even personal information. While some might have characterized this process as self-serving, I would beg to differ. We certainly learned a great deal at those mealtime meetings, but in most cases the information was utilized to enable Clark to better serve these clients, his community, and his company. Never once did I hear of any betrayal of confidences or improper use of information gained at one of those lunches

Lawyers tend to be much better talkers than listeners. Law schools teach them how to speak but fail to mention effective listening skills. I was inclined no differently. But as I observed Clark, first listening, then asking probing questions, I found myself striving to emulate him. I wanted to listen to understand, not necessarily to respond. Suddenly my questions became more important than my answers.

It is curious that the simple act of listening can be such a gift. It rarely results in a profound solution but perhaps there is a talking cure if only someone will listen. This is biblical as well—one of God's greatest gifts to us is his willingness to tirelessly listen to us. As I practice this with David or Carson (or as they listen to me), I am able to effectively communicate care and acceptance. They feel understood—even if I can't assist in the actual solving of the problem. It enables a cathartic process or unburdening to occur and trust to be built. Listening has truly built a bridge between our worlds and, in the process, David and I have both felt more loved and accepted.

Listening Is Good . . . but Look for Clues before You Respond

By giving others our full attention as they speak to us, we are not only more likely to understand what they are trying to tell us, but we also give respect and honor to the friendship or relationship. Every relationship would benefit by this, but sometimes respect and sensitivity only happen once we make a conscious change in our patterns of relating to others. I've wrestled with this problem personally, but I've discovered that both these qualities come more readily when I take time to utilize the following simple steps:

1. *Observe* what's happening to others.
2. *Consider* their needs and feelings.
3. *Respond* with appropriate words and actions.

1. *Observe.* Many of us wander through life oblivious to the feelings and needs of others. But if we are observant, we can learn to be aware of how others are feeling by noticing their body language. It doesn't take much study to perceive whether someone is relaxed and comfortable or uptight and fidgety. As we read the signs we can adjust how we approach that person. These same observational skills need to be practiced in our interaction with friends. If someone's body language changes or if the person doesn't seem quite himself, we should take the time to ask why.

2. *Consider.* The second step is to consider what we do and how it may affect others. That is, we need to pay attention to how others' feelings and/or needs are affected by what we say and do. A classic *Harvard Business Review* article explains how we can get insights into others' emotions by listening to what they say through their "word metaphors."[2] For example, if a colleague says he "struck out" with a particular client, we can deduce that business for him today feels like a baseball game. He may be discouraged, but it still feels like good, healthy competition. On the other hand, if he says, he was "blown out of the water," he may be feeling more like he is at war. He may be disappointed but might also feel afraid or fearful about his livelihood. I wouldn't attempt to read too much into such phrases, but they can give us terrific insight into how others are feeling.

3. *Respond.* By choosing to take into account how others appear through their body language, the words they use and what we already know about their feelings, we can adjust our words and behaviors to be more sensitive in how we respond. There is one particular time that I recall using these three elements in an attempt to assist an employee. I was sitting at my desk, at one

of our family company's division offices. By just glancing up, I could see most of our managers as they arrived at work and walked past my office door. However, as it often is in a busy office, everyone was eager to get a jump on the day's projects, so they would rarely stop to greet me in the morning.

One day, I looked up as a coworker passed by my office. I noticed that his body language seemed different somehow. He seemed stooped and heavy, and just looking at him made me wonder if something was wrong. I followed him to his office and asked if everything was all right. At first, he put up a brave front, but I wasn't convinced. In fact, even as he talked, I could sense that he was hurting. I gently probed further. He then broke down and told me that his teenage daughter had just run away from home! We ended up talking at great length, and I was able to offer him some support and encouragement.

After *observing* this man's body language as he walked by my office door, I chose to act on that observation and take time to listen to him. I then *considered* his specific needs. Based on both my observations and my considerations of his needs as I talked to him. Lastly, I was able to *respond* with a word of encouragement and some support. There was nothing elaborate about what I did; it was three simple steps that any of us can take. But in choosing to take those steps, I made a significant difference to one man's life. It also served as a good reminder to me to be more observant of others, especially those close to me.

Conclusion

Well-known counselor and author Dr. Larry Crabb says, "Speaking is the gateway to relationship. Silence is the gatekeeper."[3] Transformational friendships require that men truly listen to one another with sensitivity and respect. Carson, Bob, and I have been able to do that by habitually taking time to *observe* how we are doing, taking time to *consider* what impact our words might have on one another, and then carefully adjusting our *responses* to reflect what we have heard and observed.

These important skills have benefited our covenant relationship, but they are applicable to other relationships as well. Taking time to respond works to build trust in any relationship.

I admit that I used to be a selfish listener and focused most of my conversational energy on preparing what I wanted to say. However, I have discovered how wonderful it is when others listen deeply to me. As a consequence, I am trying to actively develp this skill, whether it is in discussions with my wife, family, friends, or business associates.

Why not take some time to *listen* to a friend today?

Everyone should be quick to listen... slow to speak.

—James 1:19

Chapter 10

Are Your Secrets Safe with a Friend?

Covenant of Confidentiality: I will promise to keep confidential whatever is shared within the confines of our mutual covenant in order to protect the atmosphere of openness and trust.

"Loose lips sink ships." This is a common expression we have all heard, typically with little thought given to the battleships and lives lost as a result of careless speech. The expression originated in World War II and reminds us that passing on too much information can have a deadly result. Our words today don't typically influence military outcomes, but careless words can still sink friendships.

Think back to when you were in elementary school. Can you visualize kids whispering to each other at the edge of the playground during recess? If you were smart, you probably trusted only your closest friends with your most important secrets. It was even deemed a sign of a special friendship if you had someone with whom you shared a secret. Perhaps you also remember how disappointed you were when you discovered that you couldn't rely on some of those friends to keep your secrets. As I mentioned in chapter 2, making friends at Harvard involved the same principles we utuilized on the playground. In this chapter, we will see that both school children and the world's most successful businesspeople share a common need for trusted friends and confidants.

We All Need Confidants

For seven years, I was a member of the Young Presidents Organization (YPO), a worldwide association with annual conferences that feature unparalleled educational and training experiences for its members. Over the years, 75 percent of members surveyed have consistently said that the highlight of their association with YPO is not the travel, exotic as it always is, nor was it the connection with both universities and academics, as great as they both were. Instead, the most significant, and most memorable aspect of this association was the opportunity to participate in a forum group. This is a group of eight or ten members who met monthly to share business and personal challenges and to offer and receive support.

The continued success of the forum groups is widely attributed to the assurance of confidentiality by its members.[1] This confidentiality provides an environment where transparency can thrive, confidences can be shared, and personal lessons learned. In turn, this enables a highly valued experience for these successful business leaders.

Just as children thrive when they have a trusted friend, so do adults. The continued success of forum groups further points to the growing recognition by men that there is a need for male friendship in the adult years and that there is a benefit to gathering together to provide mutual support and encouragement. It may be easier for some men to initiate this type of relationship within a business context, where the challenges of business are common and less personal. Significantly, many of us have a tendency to believe (or act as though we believe) that our problems and issues are unique, and this can be an obstacle to disclosure. Yet once we speak our innermost thoughts, we inevitably discover that our fears and concerns are more common than we think.

I'm not suggesting that we begin to make everything in our lives a confidential matter to discuss exclusively with the boys. But it can be most helpful at times. In addition, for those of us who are married, our spouses should be the confidants with whom we share life's most private and important details. However, if you are having difficulty in your marriage and need someone to help you to honor your lifelong commitment to your partner, it may help to have a friend to whom you can turn to in confidence.

My wife, Alison, is in full agreement with my having male confidants with whom I can speak—even about our marriage. She says: "When we are struggling in our relationship, David's friends have helped him to work things through, and I am confident they do so in a way that is supportive of our marriage. I never worry about David talking to his covenant partners about us. In fact, when things get really tough, I almost prefer that he talk first to Carson and Bob."

Be Careful What You Say

A few years ago, Alison and I began discussing the idea of buying a larger home with a pool and more room for our teenaged kids and their friends. Ultimately, this led to us considering purchasing my parents' house. I had discussed the idea with my mom and dad a few years earlier, when they began to think about moving into a smaller residence. Alison liked their home, and I told my mom and dad that if it was ever helpful to them or should they ever want to put their property on the market, we would be interested in purchasing it.

Two years later, my mother was diagnosed to be terminally ill with cancer. This was her third bout with the disease and, over dinner, I explained to our children that their grandmother was not expected to live much longer. Our oldest, Christy, (fourteen years-old at the time) was quick to ask, "What will Grandpa do?" He was advanced in years and struggling with Alzheimer's disease. She recognized that without my mom, he would obviously need some assistance. I responded by asking what she thought he should do. Her immediate reply was, "He should live with us."

Over dinner our family discussed this possibility, and we all agreed that our home would be too small for all of us if my dad moved in. We then made a family decision to offer to live with dad and care for him if he ended up being alone. I mentioned this to Carson and Bob, as well as the earlier discussions about buying my mom and dad's house. I wasn't certain that I should raise the subject early on with my family, given that mom's condition was still somewhat unpredictable. From my perspective,

I reasoned that I could save heartache and upset for my dad and my siblings by advising them ahead of time that we would be there to help out. However, both Bob and Carson suggested that I wait until my mom's situation was clarified. It could be presumptuous as well as upsetting to my family to bring up discussions about mom's death or the sale of the family home. I heeded their advice and, in retrospect, I think it was wise.

My wonderful mom died two months later on Christmas Day. I was with her at the time, holding her hand, while my brother did the same across the bed from me. Mom, or "Gammy" as we called her, was a loving, giving, and energetic woman right until the end. She was an unselfish and thoughtful woman, who often went out of her way to make her children happy. I remember, when I was five years old, and she agreed to buy a red Pontiac convertible because she wanted to support my childhood dreams of being a fireman. (If you think I was spoiled as a child, you are probably right!)

Almost immediately after mom died, I talked with my siblings about our family's willingness to be with dad, at least temporarily. We acted on this and "bunked in" with dad within days of mom's passing. At the memorial service, my dad told me that he would like Alison and me to have his home.

Typically, I am very open, so I immediately shared with my sisters and brothers dad's suggestion, and I also explained that the idea had been discussed years earlier. Unfortunately, everyone's emotions were a bit raw and, for a host of other reasons, this discussion brought discomfort and upset to the broader family, even though everyone wanted the best for our father.

One of my sisters indicated that our actions seemed hasty. I assured her that we were not acting impulsively. In fact, I reminded her that this had been the subject of consideration for several years. I should have left it at that. However, in my eagerness to prove the point, I explained that I had talked to both Bob and Carson about this months earlier and that they had advised me not to discuss it with the family until it was necessary to do so.

Wrong! Without thinking, I had unwittingly breached the confidence of my friendship by telling my sister how they had advised me. This may seem innocuous, but the next Sunday at church, Bob felt uncomfortable when he saw my sister. I had told him about her response, and now he knew that she knew. He was now caught up in our family dynamic.

Why hadn't I just said, "Alison and I thought about it a couple of months earlier"? After all, we were both unified in our desire to care for dad and our family knew that. My tendency to defer to someone else's opinion rather than stating my own is probably what led me to mention Bob and Carson's advice. This without thinking about the impact it could have on Bob's relationship with my family. In hindsight, I can see how someone might have thought I was scheming with my lawyer as how to take advantage of the situation and get a favorable deal.

As it turned out, everyone was happy about the arrangements in the end. Moreover, I had learned an important lesson along the way. Unfortunately it caused a short-term and unnecessary disruption in my relationships.

Guard Others' Words

Although openness, vulnerability, and honesty are vitally important to relationships, it is even more important that we learn to guard confidential information entrusted to us by others. As the biblical writer puts it, "to everything there is a season," including "a time for speaking and a time to refrain from speaking" (Ecclesiastes 3:1, 7).

To illustrate this, let me again explain a situation where I might have made a wiser choice about what to say. One day, I told my wife, Alison, about an opinion that Carson had expressed to me in confidence. It was related to my own life and, frankly, I tell Alison almost everything, as is appropriate for a married couple. But this was a case where I didn't need to identify Carson as the source of the advice. Later, she unwittingly repeated my comments to Carson's wife, Brenda, along with the words, "I can't believe Carson said that." Fortunately, Alison went on to say that she felt Carson was right and appreciated his perspective. However, if Alison hadn't thought his comments appropriate, my slip might easily have damaged the trusting relationship that Alison has experienced for more than twenty-five years with both Carson and Brenda.

I am learning that the less I say about what other people have said privately, the better. As a general rule, I now strive to use the phrase "I've been thinking"—instead of naming others and labeling their opinion. Confidential information should be strictly regarded as such (and not shared as a way to build alliances). If we fail to honor confidences, our friends will soon begin to hold back on what they share with us.

Safeguards

The best safeguard for confidentiality is the trustworthy character of your friend(s). Choosing with whom you share confidences is a matter of judgment. Obviously, not everyone can be trusted, so prudence would suggest that we not share intimate details of our lives with those whose character is unknown to us. Additionally, it is helpful to be clear about what information is confidential and what can be shared. In a group I formerly belonged to, we had an explicit standard of confidentiality: "Nothing, nobody, never." This meant that whenever we were in doubt about whether we could share anything confidential, this standard would provide clear direction. There were no exceptions. In order to ensure this high standard was honored, we began each meeting with a reminder of this expression and that any breach of it was grounds for removal from the group.

Similarly, in our covenant we have solemnly declared our promise to honor confidential information as such. Being explicit is vital, and it never hurts to remind or emphasize to your friends what your expectations are regarding confidentiality.

Over time, as you and your friends each share confidences, you will have the added benefit of reciprocity to guard your private information. Personally, I find it helps me to trust someone else with my innermost secrets or feelings when I know that they have already done so with me.

Conclusion

If this discussion of vulnerability and confidentially sounds unrealistic or frightening, I would encourage you to start slowly. Find a friend you trust, and disclose to him a need or concern with which he may be able to assist you. Tell him that you want to learn to trust him, and emphasize the significance of confidentiality to both of you. Little by little, relational trust can be earned—and learned. As our friends prove dependable with small things, we may gain confidence to trust them with our very souls. "It is a good thing to find one man or a couple of men . . . with whom you can be fully open, someone with whom you can walk side by side . . . with no secrets between you."[2]

Gossip separates the best of friends.

—Proverbs 16:28, *Living Bible*

Chapter 11

Who Checks Up on You?

Covenant of Accountability: I covenant to use the gifts that God has given me for your benefit. If I discover areas of my life that are negatively affected by my own misdoings or by the scars inflicted by others, I will seek Christ's liberating power through His Holy Spirit and through you so that I might better serve God and fulfill my covenants to you. I am accountable to you in my commitment to become what God has designed me to be in his loving creation.

It's late at night and I miss my family—especially my wife. I'm alone in a hotel room and the adult-only selections on the television call to me softly and seductively. I reason to myself that no one will ever know if I choose to watch an erotic film; after all, it wouldn't hurt anyone . . . would it?

Psychologist Larry Crabb says that all men "understand the allure of sex."[1] Unfortunately, so do movie-makers, book publishers, and magazine sellers. As a result we now "live in a world awash with sensual images available twenty-four hours a day in a variety of mediums."[2] It's a rare man who doesn't struggle, at least in some way, with sexual temptation. One of my friends wrote the following about his dance with temptation during a business trip to Asia:

I spotted the girl the way you spot a red rose in an otherwise black-and-white picture. She swung into the airport lounge, all beauty and charisma, talking in an animated way to her companions. My mind seemed to immediately determine that she would be the focus of my attention for the next few hours, and I hastily committed to the ride. I'd been resolutely faithful to my wife and had no intention of being unfaithful, yet I still thought I was able to play a reckless game of temptation and not be beaten.

She wore perfume, I noticed. Was that for me? There was no awkwardness in asking her to sit beside me—because she asked first. Before I knew it, she was helping me buckle my seatbelt, something I'd always felt capable of handling myself before. When we landed, she offered to chauffeur me to my hotel, and by the time we reached it, we'd arranged to meet that evening. My business didn't start until the next day, and I reasoned that book learning never supplanted what you could find out from the locals. I might learn something about the local investment climate or perhaps gain access to information and people to which I'd never otherwise come close. It seemed like a fair justification.

We went for dinner and found a club with great dance music. It felt intoxicating and all too soon, midnight had come and gone. We hailed a taxi, and as she squeezed as close as possible next to me, I spoke of my wife back home—it was a weakening shield against the power of her shapely body, draped with long black hair.

Did she want to meet again? She just nodded. She moved to kiss me on the lips, but I reluctantly turned so that my cheek received the memorable caress. I left the cab, turned and waved, and scrambled to my room. No, I wasn't going to sleep any time soon. My body was on fire for her and my mind led the charge. When I finally fell asleep, clothes still on, it was 4 A.M.

The alarm shrilled at 7:30 A.M. to begin what was supposed to be a day of business for my largest client. But I had something more important to do.

Grabbing my electronic pocket diary, I plugged in the name of one of my buddies from the men's Bible study group with whom I'd met weekly over the past three years. For the most part, the friendships had grown around a common faith and a mutual commitment to a meaningful friendship. I needed that friendship now. I was calling just one of them, but really it didn't matter which one. I knew they would all be there for me—to act as the powerful shield that I could have used the night before. I needed one of my buddies to point me back in the right direction.

I couldn't reach one, nor another...nor another. No luck, but—and this is tough to explain—by the time I'd got the third phone number, I didn't even need to dial it. Just the act of acknowledging the authority my friends had over me and my marriage had brought back into play all the weaponry that God puts at our disposal when temptation rears its ugly head. Never before had the following verse appeared so meaningful to me: "No temptation has overtaken you that is not common to man. God is faithful and He will not let you be tempted beyond your strength, but with the temptation will also provide the way of escape, that you may be able to endure it." (1 Corinthians 10:13)

Why Be Accountable in Friendship?

We all experience temptation, yet how many of us have someone to talk to about it—that is, other than a priest or a rabbi or a paid counselor? When faced with a need for someone to help you with problems, it's very easy to rationalize that issues aren't significant enough to warrant setting an appointment to consult with a church leader or a paid counselor. So most of us don't do anything about it; we just soldier on alone, hoping we will work it out over time. There is, however, another solution, one that is, perhaps, even more likely to succeed: That is to anticipate problems before they arise, to steel ourselves against them by creating friendships dedicated to transformation, and then becoming prepared to be accountable for our actions and our responses to temptation.

The word *accountable* means being subject to the obligation to report, explain, or justify something. To be accountable is to be responsible or answerable to someone else. When you consider the weightiness of this definition, it's no wonder that so few people are willing to make themselves accountable to others! I have chosen to be accountable to Bob and Carson, and this means that in our covenant friendship we talk about issues with which I (and they) need help. In particular, our discussions have helped me develop strategies to deal with both sexual temptation and anger.

I have to confess that on the night described at the beginning of this chapter, I didn't make the best choice in terms of what movie I watched. More recently, however, before leaving on a trip to California, I discussed my late-night movie temptations with Carson and Bob. One of them suggested that I develop a proactive strategy to avoid falling into this trap. The best—and simplest—solution was for me to ask the front desk clerk to block the adult movie stations when I first checked into the hotel. Frankly, I don't like to do this because it's embarrassing for a grown man to make such a request. Yet knowing that I would be held accountable to Carson and Bob enabled me to get past this discomfort quite quickly. After all, facing a raised eyebrow from an unknown hotel desk clerk can be much easier than facing the raised eyebrows and direct questions of close friends. An added bonus is that I think I may have left the hotel clerk wondering about my desire for self-discipline and moral purity.

This simple strategy involved making a deliberate choice to be accountable for my actions and then taking a practical step to overcome temptation. Nothing fancy, but as a result I have discovered a strategy to successfully avoid viewing sexually explicit material.

This is just one example of how mutual accountability has helped me. It is interesting that we tend to ignore the benefits of accountability in our personal lives, even though we expect—and typically face—accountability for our conduct in our professional lives, families, and communities. There is usually a supervisor or board of directors or even shareholders who call us to account at work. At home, most of us understand that we are accountable to our families and our wives, at least in terms of how we spend our time and money. In our communities we have professional associations and churches that add their own set of expectations to how we lead our lives. In our more lucid moments, we readily acknowledge that these expectations are helpful and lead us to greater success in building business, family, and community. So why are most of us still reluctant to accept the notion of accountability in our personal lives?

Our Reluctance to Accept Accountability

Self-Reliance

Perhaps it is because Western society applauds men who display independence and self-reliance, and we encourage young men to attain these qualities. There is nothing wrong with these qualities; in fact, in and of themselves they are quite admirable. However, without the counterbalancing influence of qualities such as restraint and discipline, our selfish appetites have the potential to transform independence and self-reliance into destructive behaviors. Pursuing our own agendas may have some positive outcomes. Yet more than likely it will prevent us from giving adequate consideration to those whom we care most about and, ultimately, harm both our working and personal relationships.

Our Tendency to Image Build

Many men work hard to create a strong, positive public image. For some it's an image of power, buttressed by the positions they hold. For others, it's an image of financial success, reinforced by the possessions they have. For still others, it's a moral or religious image that is polished by acts of charity or devotion.

The ironic thing about striving to attain a certain image is that underneath the façade we remain aware that our weaknesses, problems, and emotions are still present. There's also an accompanying inner fear that our public image will be shattered if we slip up and somehow let our true selves become known. So we hide beneath the image we have created. Eventually we may become truly unable to face who we really are. As an example, I think of my dad, who was very successful in his business career. His company became substantial by most standards, yet he always resisted creating a formal board of directors. Why was that, I wonder? I think it was, in part, because he enjoyed a reputation that may have eclipsed the reality of the company. His persona may have led people to think of both him and the company as being larger than they were. My dad was a great man but, like most of us, he resisted accountability because he feared what people might think if they knew the *real* story and were privy to his weaknesses, as well as his strengths.

Our Resistance to Change

If you are like me, there is a wide gulf between your commitment to excellence in your career and to that in your personal life. We are willing to attend seminars to learn better job-related skills or strategies. Yet, in our personal lives we seem quite content to sing that same old tune, "I can't change—that's just the way I am."

Let's face it—change is uncomfortable—even positive change. Instead we tend to plod along in our personal lives, content with mediocrity (or worse), until we are prompted or forced by circumstance to change. This reality is reflected in the Alcoholics Anonymous Twelve-Step recovery program. It acknowledges that a key step to living a better life is to "admit that our lives have become unmanageable." Sadly, too often it is only when we recognize that we are in way over our heads, that we reach out for the assistance and advice of others. We don't need to be out of control to recognize this. Rather, we need to be mature enough to examine our lives and realize they can be enhanced and made more manageable with the input and help of others.

Reasons to Accept Accountability in Our Lives

Discrepancies between Our Intentions and What We Do

Some people believe that accountability isn't necessary if you are strong or disciplined enough as a person. If this is true, why are personal fitness trainers in such demand? After all, some argue that it makes little sense to pay money to have someone else to help you exercise. They reason that if you are determined enough, you should be able to motivate yourself and exercise on your own. Yet increasing numbers of adults are now entering into accountability relationships with trainers because they know that such a relationship will enable them to perform at a higher level than they could if left to their own initiative.

Moreover, most of us already know what we should be doing to improve our lives. But when it comes to actually doing what we need to do, we fall short. There is typically a huge discrepancy between our good intentions and our actions so we turn to teachers, coaches, and managers to help us to bridge that gap.

One day I noted a newspaper picture of tennis star Venus Williams standing beside her coach, Billie Jean King. Williams had just won the U.S. Open Women's Doubles Championship, and the photograph made me wonder how well King would do against Williams in a tennis match today. Since King is more than twice Williams's age, such a match is not likely. Yet this illustrates the concept that coaches don't have to be better at something to effectively encourage others to achieve their best.

Today, both personal life coaching and executive coaching have become very popular. For a fee, you can hire a private coach who will provide you guidance on a regular basis. They will enable you to make your life more manageable and assist you in achieving your goals.

However, we don't always have the luxury, or even the need, to hire such professionals, because friendship has the same potential to encourage and enable us to better ourselves. The observations, feedback, and encouragement of friends aren't commercially motivated, but they can be every bit as beneficial. It is critical to success in helping a friend to have a sense of accountability. Not surprisingly, the success of accountability in relationships with trainers relies on some of the principles of friendship. That is, we generally expect a coach to treat us as an ideal friend—looking out for our best interests and assisting us in attaining our goals.

Setting Goals

When Bob and I first began meeting together, our primary purpose was to remind each other about the areas in our lives in which we wanted to experience growth. Years later, I still have lots of room to grow in most of these areas and, perhaps, that will be the case for my whole life. But as I look back, I am particularly grateful that my accountability relationship with Bob pushed me to succeed in one significant life goal—to spend more time with my mom and dad.

My mom died when I was forty, and my father slipped into the confused world of Alzheimer's disease soon after. Thankfully, I can look back with little regret, knowing that as she aged, I made time for my mom, periodically taking her out for a lunch date or dropping by for tea. Similarly, as I mentioned in the introduction, I had lunch with my dad at least two days a week for a period of several years. While this served our business interests as he mentored me in the family business and introduced me to many of his business associates, the central purpose of these meetings was my desire to honor him and to be with him.

Taking time with mom and dad was a key priority for me. I was motivated to accomplish it partly because I knew that each week Bob would be asking me if I had taken time for my parents. I can only imagine the regrets I would have today had Bob not kept me accountable to accomplishing this important goal.

We Need Help Getting Issues on the Table

Some people argue that developing a relationship of mutual support and accountability comes more easily for women, who possess maternal, nurturing characteristics that enable them to articulate their feelings more easily.

But men also have natural tendencies that can help them in pursuing genuine friendship. For example, the typically male quality of being frank or direct in conversation may be an advantage in probing beneath the emotional surface, getting issues on the table quickly, and then dealing with them constructively. In other words, although women may find it easier to share their need for accountability, men may find it easier to speak the words that actually hold one another accountable.

As I have consulted with families who share business interests, I have observed examples of these different tendencies between men and women. Typically, the women in the family are more likely to see the need for regular family meetings to discuss issues and to ensure that everyone is informed and following through on what needs to get done. However, in the meetings themselves, women are more apt to be quiet, and the men tend to be more direct in bringing up issues for discussion. (Not all families follow this pattern, but I have seen this enough times to conclude that it does seem to be a common pattern.)

How to Create Accountability Relationships

Choose Accountability Partners Carefully

Not every friend will be an effective accountability partner. Some friends may not be willing to confront you, and others may simply be more interested in having a good time together than working toward goals together. Dr. Howard Hendricks, a professor at Dallas Theological Seminary, recommends that accountability partners be selected based on the following criteria:

1. They appreciate you and your gifts but haven't put you on a pedestal.
2. You have affected their lives and they appreciate your influence, but they are not intimidated by you or your accomplishments.
3. They love and accept you—yet love you too much to allow you to remain as you are. That is, they care enough about you to want you to grow, develop, and work on some of the bad habits that keep you from a full enjoyment of life.[3]

As psychologist Larry Crabb writes, "If the connection consists of profound acceptance, looking for the good, and the ability to see bad without retreating, then friendship exists."[4]

Give Rights to Accountability Partners

Dr. Hendricks suggests that we give accountability partners the following four rights: the right to question, the right to evaluate, the right to rebuke, and the right to counsel. In the following paragraphs, I outline how we have applied each of these points to our covenant relationship.

The Right to Question

Invite friends to question you about your progress towards your life goals and/or values. This is the basis of all accountability. For example, I am a mentor with an organization called Virtus. Periodically, all participants in this peer-mentoring program are invited to write out their most important personal and work-related goals. These goals are then exchanged with one other member of the group. In these pairs, each individual has the opportunity to invite his partner to check up on his progress. Because each of us has chosen our own objectives (they are not imposed on us) and because we voluntarily invite a friend to follow up, mutual accountability becomes a very powerful tool to bring about change.

The success of mutual accountability is at least partly due to pride. No one likes to be seen by others as not having carried through with their intentions. That is, mutual accountability actually motivates us to work harder at achieving our goals, just so we can avoid the discomfort of failing in the eyes of others.

The Right to Evaluate

This right creates the potential for others to look beyond your words to determine what is really going on. For example, if I say that I am doing fine and getting sufficient rest, my friends might notice the bags under my eyes and, therefore, believe they have reason to probe further. This isn't necessarily a search for lies or deceptions. In many cases, the person may be genuinely attempting to answer the question honestly but may be too close to the situation to accurately recognize what is really happening in his life.

The Right to Rebuke

This right is a stronger intervention than evaluating words and body language. For example, if I had not found time to be with my children or my wife for an extended period of time because I was too busy water-skiing every day, my friends might choose to rebuke me. In doing so they would remind me of my priorities and my responsibilities. They might even choose to do this with some firmness.

Many would shrink from this kind of encounter, fearing that a rebuke would be judgmental and potentially harmful to the friendship. While there is that risk, the situation can be properly navigated and the friendship strengthened if: 1) the person being rebuked has invited this kind of accountability; and 2) the person doing the rebuking is doing so with sensitivity and without malice.

Most of us would never consider going to a friend's house for dinner without an invitation. Even so, when invited, we are not likely to throw open the door, waltz in, and tell our host to repaint the living room. Accountability is somewhat similar; it requires not only sensitivity and invitation but also a good sense of timing.

The Right to Counsel

This right includes the privilege of offering suggestions to others as to what might be an appropriate action in a given circumstance. This may be contrary to some of today's popular philosophies that discourage us from offering counsel to another. That is, we each possess everything we need to be all that we can be. This common but mistaken belief implies that we each have all we need for life and success. Yet in so believing, it also perpetuates the belief that we have nothing to offer others and that others have nothing to offer to us. In contrast, I maintain that even if you have within you all the potential in the world, the wise counsel of others can always enhance it.

It may be difficult to think of giving your friends the right to counsel, yet by doing so, we offer them an opportunity to share insights into our lives that no amount of introspection could ever yield.

Submit to One Another

Submission is another element of mutual accountability. If you or I pay a trainer to guide us in an exercise program, then we have made a deliberate choice to submit to the trainer's instruction; the trainer hasn't just arbitrarily decided that we need his or her assistance and barged into our lives! We asked the trainer into our lives, and we have the power to opt out, even in the middle of a workout. When a trainer is standing beside us and encouraging us as we work out, though, we rarely choose that option. Rather, we are more likely to find that extra strength and desire that we need to continue—no matter how much it hurts.

The primary responsibility in an accountability relationship belongs to the one who has chosen to submit to another. For example, if I asked Carson and Bob to hold me accountable to having regular dates with each of my four children, then their primary role is to remind me and encourage me to do so. After that, it is up to me to act. I learned, the hard way, how important this is because of what happened when I once forgot to give Bob an opportunity to submit to my input. On that occasion, I was so focused on keeping him accountable that I hassled him rather than allowed him to respond.

The three of us were on a retreat and Bob used this opportunity to confess that he was finding life overwhelming and his schedule grossly overextended. I probed deeper by asking him whether he was working on Sundays or taking time for a Sabbath day off. Bob was honest and explained that he was not taking a weekly day of rest. I was concerned and felt this was unwise. He was running himself down physically, and I was sure that he was on the road to burnout. Furthermore, he was not obeying the biblical command to take one day of rest each week.

I decided that I wasn't going to let him continue with this pattern. I wanted Bob to change the way he was managing his life and, in particular, how he was spending his Sundays. I had talked to him about this subject previously, so he was quite familiar with my opinion. However, I was now determined to challenge him until he made some changes. Much to my surprise, as I began to press the issue, Bob burst into tears.

He tried to explain that he was already feeling overwhelmed, and that when he had confessed his struggles, he felt that I had attacked him and made it worse. He also thought I had tried to control his behavior and tell him what he should do. As Bob explained how I had hurt him, he noted that he didn't need me to add more pressure to his already overstressed life.

In my defense, I explained that I wasn't trying to apply pressure, I simply saw that he was doing something that I believed was wrong and that he probably also knew was wrong. I then added that, as his accountability partner, I only wanted to help him get back to a more balanced life. I also told him that if he saw me doing something wrong, I would want him to hang me up by fingernails to stop me from doing it. My attempt to clarify my motives only served to open the floodgates further. Bob sobbed, and through his tears he told me that the last thing he needed was for me to "hang him up by his fingernails!" He said he needed grace, love, and support. He did not need my judgment and pressure. Suddenly, I felt foolish and very embarrassed.

Bob forgave me that night but, in retrospect, this experience demonstrates a vitally important principle of accountability—it is about follow through, not about judging or controlling. Calling others to account, as the word suggests, is best thought about more in terms of voluntary submission, rather than in terms of supervision. I have learned that the best approach to accountability is to come alongside our brothers, remind them of their commitments, and encourage them with our love.

In hindsight, I should have first entered into a discussion with Bob by asking more questions about what was going on in his life. His remarks would likely have made it clear that Bob was in desperate need of encouragement, not criticism or judgment.

"When we become judge, we stand *over* a friend. This is diametrically opposed to the position of friends, where each stands *beside* the other."[5] In other words, even when we have been invited to question, evaluate, rebuke, or counsel a friend, we are wise to do so as a peer, never from a position of superiority or criticism.

Confront One Another with Care

A slightly different approach than discussed thus far may be appropriate if we suspect that a friend is about to do something destructive or dangerous (which could result in harm to himself or others). In this situation, we have an obligation to speak up—even if our opinion is not solicited.

I'll never forget an occasion when I went to speak to a close friend (not one of my covenant partners) about a significant issue in his life. I had reason to believe that he was having an affair, and I knew this would have a disastrous effect not only on his own marriage and family but also on the family of the woman in question. I didn't know for sure that there was an affair, but I felt that the evidence was strong enough that I should talk to him. I prayed a lot, and then I planned a strategy that I hoped would preserve our friendship regardless of whether or not my hunch was correct.

I met with him privately, on neutral ground, and shared with him a specific example of when I had struggled with temptation in my life. I endeavored to be truly empathetic and told him that regardless of whether he had or hadn't committed adultery, I still wanted to be his friend. I told him that I wanted the best for him. This involved expressing my support for him while, at the same time, asking him to take a look in the mirror and make sure that his life was consistent with the kind of person he wanted to be.

As it turned out, my hunch was wrong. Thankfully, our friendship was preserved—and even strengthened—because he was grateful that I hadn't judged him, and yet had cared enough about him to risk the conversation.

Conclusion

Socrates said that "an unexamined life is not worth living."[6] He was right, and our friends can be invaluable in helping us to examine our lives truthfully and then to take the steps necessary for change. The key to a successful accountability relationship between friends is to voluntarily submit to one another rather than to stand over each other in judgment. If you have never experienced the healthy, growth-inducing impact that can come from accountability in a mutual friendship, then I challenge you to start practicing accountability in your friendships.

> *Better is open rebuke than hidden love. A wound from a friend can be trusted.*
>
> —Proverbs 27:5–6a, NIV

Part III

How Friendship Helps

As our covenant friendship has transformed the workings of our "inner selves," we have found that all areas of our lives have been similarly enhanced. As we have grown in confidence and learned to listen and to speak openly, we have become better able to respond to the people and situations that surround us. Our marriages have improved, our parenting skills have benefited, and our relationships with our children have grown deeper. As we actively work to improve each of these areas we have experienced positive, tangible benefits.

Friendship, especially covenant friendship, is transformational. We have experienced its life-changing impact in the following areas:

1. Our marriages
2. Our parenting
3. Our careers
4. Our fitness levels
5. Our thinking
6. Our spirits

The next six chapters explore and illustrate how our covenant friendships have influenced and enhanced each of these areas in our lives.

Chapter 12

Helping Me Love My Spouse

Marriage is a delight, a comfort, an inspiration, and an adventure. It's a wonderful gift from God, and at times it's exhilarating. It's all of these things and much more, but one thing it often is *not* easy. In fact, if you want to build a marriage that will last, you are likely in for a battle, especially because we live in a culture that is at "war against the family."[1]

Whether through the law, entertainment, or even the over-exaggerated emphasis on tolerance, our society celebrates and endorses sexuality but seldom marriage. In recent years, statistics consistently show that nearly one out of every two marriages in North America ends in divorce. Commonly, the chances are only fifty-fifty that your marriage will merely survive. Yet, despite such dismal odds—or perhaps because of such dismal odds—Bob, Carson, and I have made a decision that we will actively work to create and maintain marriages that are healthy, dynamic, fulfilling, and meaningful. As friends, we are committed to help each other to accomplish this.

Alison and I have been married for more than twenty-five years and, during that time, we've read plenty of marital self-help books, received the advice and support of some terrific marriage counselors, and attended some perceptive seminars. In addition, we've discovered that our friends can be very effective in supporting us and helping us shield our marriage from the many attacks it faces, both from within and without. The accountability and sustained encouragement of committed friends has proven to be extremely valuable to us as we learn about love and the practicalities of married life.

As covenant friends, Bob, Carson, and I routinely take time to talk about our marriages and to discuss the issues that we face in loving our wives. In our conversations, we actively strive to help each other work through issues in a way that is beneficial to our spouses and to our marriages. My friends have helped me to recognize areas in my life that needed to change so our marriage could progress; they have been supportive at times when Alison and I have found ourselves in a relational crisis; and they have helped me to take a step forward when I felt unsure about what to do next. They have held me accountable to making time with Alison a priority, and they have upheld and endorsed my efforts to become a better husband.

Blind Spots

Just as the retina of the human eye contains a blind spot, so too the human soul contains a blind spot. Soul friends can help us see things we cannot see on our own. . . . The true soul friend will not accept our self-deceptions but will gently and firmly confront us with our soul blindness.[2]

We all have blind spots—those places where we can't see our personal faults or issues clearly. They impact our lives, relationships, and careers. They are particularly vexing in a marriage relationship, where even the smallest details are exposed over time. Chances are that our spouses not only clearly see our blind spots but, more often than not, also suffer the consequences of their existence. As David Benner states above, our closest friends can play a key role in helping us to recognize and deal with the blind spots that impact our lives and our marriages. We may not like it, but sometimes we must trust the perspective of friends to help us recognize or acknowledge the hurtful or negative things that we don't see in our own hearts, actions, and words.

Consider the following example, the story of my friend Jeff, who served as a missionary to Africa for ten years. He was married to Sharon, a wonderful woman who he dearly loved and who shared his heart for missions. But, during their time in Africa, Jeff's work frequently took him away from his wife and family for extended periods of time. Due to rather primitive conditions, there was often no way for him to maintain communication with his family. To add to this stress, Jeff worked in active war zones—which meant that his family not only had to deal with silence for weeks at a time but also with the uncertainty of Jeff being safe or even alive.

Over time, as one can easily imagine, these stresses began to take their toll on Jeff's marriage. Sharon began to feel unimportant and insignificant as his travel consumed increasing amounts of his time. She single-handedly had to carry out all of the parenting responsibilities for their four children and was essentially alone in dealing with the emotional stress of knowing that Jeff's life was constantly at risk. Sharon longed to return to the United States, where she hoped that her marriage and family relationships would return to normal.

Sharon and Jeff did eventually return to the States, but things did not return to normal. Jeff still had a strong desire to be in Africa, and this feeling was reinforced as he was constantly offered new opportunities to carry out short-term projects overseas. Every time Jeff brought up the idea of returning to Africa, he unconsciously sent his wife the message that she was not his top priority—that distant country was. The problem in their marriage was obvious to Sharon, yet Jeff was completely oblivious. He thought that his wife's lack of enthusiasm for his work reflected a diminished vision for missions, and he was completely baffled by her lack of affection and love for him.

It's easy for us to see the picture clearly: Jeff was so excited about opportunities to share God's love in Africa that he failed to see that he wasn't communicating that same love to his wife at home. He saw the needs of the African people but was totally blind to the needs of his family.

Jeff's inability to see his shortcomings as a husband is hardly unique. In fact, the world is full of men like him—and I can say that, because I am one of them. As men, we tend to seek our identity and fulfillment primarily through our work and, therefore, it is where we direct most of our passion. As a result, relationships are often relegated to a lower priority. Furthermore, once a man walks down the aisle and places a ring on his wife's finger, he may mistakenly assume that the "work" in the relationship is now done. I know that I thought I could invest more time in other challenges once I had successfully "secured" a life partner.

I had no idea how self-centered I really was and seemed to be lulled into believing the fairytale promise of living happily ever after, without acknowledging the genuine effort that is required to build an enduring marriage. I suspect that Jeff and many other men probably think along the same lines at some point in their marriages.

Fortunately, Jeff had a group of close friends to whom he was committed and who were committed to upholding him and his marriage. They understood his passion for Africa, yet they could also see that it was taking him further away from his wife and family. They were able to see Jeff's blind spot, realizing that it was keeping him from fulfilling his responsibilities to his wife and family. So they gently but persuasively confronted him and encouraged him to acknowledge the need to change his life and to adjust his priorities. They suggested that he defer some of his travel so that he could spend more time with his family. In short, they not only showed him a new way of seeing things, but they also gave him the moral support to deliberately follow through with their advice.

These changes were significant, but they didn't solve all of Jeff's problems with Sharon. Spending more time at home wasn't the solution—especially since, by this time, his wife wasn't all that excited about having him around. His frequent and prolonged absences had seriously affected their ability to communicate with each other. Jeff needed to take another step to mitigate this problem. His friends encouraged him to rediscover ways and means to cherish his wife and to clearly communicate his love to her. Step by step, Jeff began to rebuild his relationship with his wife by dating her and taking the initiative to love her, just as he had during their courtship years ago. As a result, their relationship is now blossoming.

Today Jeff is the first to admit that without the help and insights of his friends, his marriage might easily have become another divorce statistic. His friends helped him to recognize his blind spots and to make better choices, such as choosing to spend more time with his wife and family. Jeff was the one who had to invest the time and effort to regain his marriage, but the perspective of friends was invaluable in initiating the badly needed changes in his life that were essential in rescuing his marriage.

Creating an Accepting Environment

As individuals it's not that difficult to find a friend with whom we enjoy spending time. On the other hand, when married couples attempt to find other couples with whom they are both compatible, it's a different story. In some instances, women don't like their husband's friends, so it's a stretch to expect them to want to spend any time together—even in an atmosphere with other couples. In other situations, both couples may get along well yet have little in common in terms of activities or interests. Consequently, it is difficult for them to be enthusiastic about doing anything together. Perhaps you are familiar with the lament, "We used to be close friends, but since they've gotten married, it's just not the same." It doesn't have to be this way.

My parents were very fortunate in belonging to a group of three couples who thoroughly enjoyed spending time together. Almost every Friday night, the other two couples would arrive at my parents' home for a quiet evening of shared laughter and conversation. Sitting beside a crackling fire in our cozy den, these six individuals built and maintained lifelong friendships as couples.

The success of their friendship was due in part to their commitment to creating and participating in shared traditions. For example, every November all six of them would squeeze three abreast into my dad's Cadillac and drive three hours from Vancouver to Seattle for a weekend of Christmas shopping. In the summer, they would holiday together on my parents' boat, and in the winter, they could invariably be found vacationing together in Palm Springs.

Yet these relationships were built on something more than shared holidays. I now understand that they provided a place of retreat for my mom and dad. When in the company of these friends, my parents were free to be themselves, without pretense and without the need to perform. In fact, I sometimes found myself embarrassed when I overheard my parents sharply disagreeing with each other in front of these couples. But as I matured, I realized that there was something healthy about this. My mom and dad didn't feel the need to pretend things were okay when they were in this environment. It was a safe place for them to be—as individuals and as a couple.

Observing these friendships over many years has convinced me that every marriage would benefit from an environment where husband and wife are accepted and mutually encouraged as a couple—in good times and in bad.

My wife and I are fortunate to have found something of this support with Bob and his wife, Renae, and with Carson and his wife, Brenda. Both couples accept Alison and me as a couple; they want us to succeed in our marriage; and they demonstrate their support through their presence in our lives, their actions, and their words of support. During the storms of life, it is of immense value to have covenant partners who, along with their spouses, are committed to accepting us as a couple and to providing us with a safe place, an environment where both Alison and I can laugh and cry and each be ourselves.

Not only have we developed strong bonds as couples, but Alison and Brenda have also formed an accountability group (similar to my friendship with Carson and Bob) with several women friends. They meet at least annually to pray for one another and their families. When I asked Alison how this accountability friendship came about, she said quite simply, "We've seen the value of this by observing you guys."

Offering Enduring Encouragement

As covenant partners, we are committed to inspiring one another to love our wives. We provide each other with emotional support when the day-to-day grind of life becomes tedious and we forget to cherish our wives, or when we temporarily lose our perspective in pursuing our goals to build lasting marriages.

One Saturday, Bob's wife, Renae, was talking over the phone with Carson's wife, Brenda, about how swamped she and Bob were feeling by the demands and busyness of everyday life. After all, Bob has a demanding career and Renae, as a mother of three, had her hands full. To illustrate her point, she mentioned that this was their wedding anniversary and they didn't even have time to celebrate it.

After Brenda hung up the phone, she and Carson quickly made a plan to ensure that Bob and Renae took at least some time for a memorable celebration. They first convinced Bob and Renae to join them for a casual dinner, using the practical approach of, "You may be busy, but you still have to eat." Carson and Brenda then scurried ahead to the restaurant and covered the simple table with a linen tablecloth and candles. When Renae and Bob arrived, this simple gesture successfully transformed a harried afternoon into a celebration of their marriage. It wasn't grandiose or time-consuming, yet this simple act created a special memory and served as a positive, marriage-building experience for everyone. It was a symbol of what friends can do to support each other in their marriages.

Bob commented, "This is typical of Carson. He is often available on five minute's notice for either of us. He's always encouraging us in our marriage, in part, by urging us to be together as a foursome. When I am away, he willingly offers his assistance with anything that my absence has made difficult. As a result, Renae views Carson not only as my friend but also, by extension, as her friend. He is someone whom she can count on if she is having a personal struggle or even if she is struggling in her relationship with me!"

Providing Support in a Crisis

Inevitably, every couple encounters some form of marital difficulty which, if not handled properly, can quickly escalate into a crisis. On several occasions, Alison and I have found ourselves in difficult situations, and we have subsequently experienced the help of our covenant friends, intervening to help us preserve our marriage.

I remember one particular occasion when we found ourselves in marital chaos. As with most crises, this one began with a small and seemingly insignificant act or word. It was Saturday morning, and we were hosting our friends for dessert and a discussion about parenting that evening. In addition, my parents were coming for a meal the next day, so we had a busy weekend of entertaining planned. There was plenty to do, and Alison asked if I could go to the store to pick up a few things.

Now, most of you probably think, as Alison did, that such a request was reasonable; after all, a loving husband would certainly see this as an opportunity to serve his wife.

I disagreed!

For twenty years, I had worked long hours and, given Alison's job as a stay-at-home mom, I didn't consider it my responsibility to shop for groceries—especially on a Saturday, when the stores are crammed wall-to-wall with shoppers. I'm sure you're thinking that I could have been a little bit more flexible—especially since we were entertaining my parents and my covenant friends. True enough.

However, as Alison knows, I am more than willing to help out around the house by tidying up or doing other things to prepare for company, I just never wanted my reward for a hard week of work to be fighting in line at the supermarket on a Saturday. The way I looked at it, Alison had all week to shop. If she chose to spend her time doing other things, that's fine, but I was not going to be the emergency shopper on weekends. In this, I suspect I may have been influenced by a small sign that sat on the desk of one of my assistants: "A lack of planning on your part does not constitute a crisis on my part."

Nonetheless, this had been a particularly busy week for Alison as she juggled our children's schedules for soccer, hockey, piano lessons, and horseback riding. There had also been orthodontic appointments, homework, three meals a day to plan and prepare, laundry, and cleaning. With all this, she just hadn't gotten around to grocery shopping. Still, from my perspective, she had also taken time to play tennis several times and to go for a run on four mornings. Therefore, when Alison asked me to shop for her, I simply said no.

As you can imagine, this started a rather heated discussion that quickly reached a crescendo. Before long our relationship was in distress. Alison and I were equally emphatic that the other's position was completely indefensible. Soon we were not speaking at all. Neither of us were willing to get past the wounds we had caused each other as the discussion had progressed.

Given this state of affairs, Alison called Carson's wife, Brenda, to say she no longer felt like having anyone over for supper.

Brenda told Carson what was happening, and he responded in classic form. He called Bob and Renae and advised them to take the night off. Then he and Brenda drove the nearly sixty minutes it takes to get to our home and plunked themselves down in our living room with the words, "We're here because we love you and we'd like to help."

Warmly and tenderly, they coaxed the story out of us. They let Alison share her frustrations first, and then they listened to mine. It was incredibly hard to listen as Alison told them what she thought about me and why. As I listened to Alison's side of the story, even I thought I sounded like a real jerk. (I can now see how frustrated Alison must have been.) But Carson and Brenda are such trusted friends that I knew they would listen fairly to me when my turn came.

Ironically, I don't even remember how we resolved what we should have done differently or even what we should do next time—that's not the point. What I do recall is that Carson led us through a process that enabled us to hear each other, then he and Brenda supported us as we reestablished communication and prayed together for guidance.

When your dryer goes on the fritz, you can always call the appliance repairman; if your muffler falls off, you know you can drop in at the shop. But take a moment to consider this: whom do you go to or whom can you call when you've had an argument that paralyzes communication between you and your mate?

Building Blocks for Enduring Relationships in Marriage

As already demonstrated, supporting friends in marriage can take on a variety of forms. On the one hand, and on a very practical and proactive level, getting together on a periodic basis for "routine check-ups" and prayer has proven to be invaluable to Carson, Bob, and me. On the other hand, the three of us meet for a retreat once or twice a year and use these longer periods of time as opportunities for deeper conversations about our marriages. The accountability questions that we typically address include:

- How is your spouse feeling about your relationship? When is the last time you asked her this question?
- How is your wife feeling about herself?
- How are you showing her you love her?
- Are you getting enough "alone time" for the two of you?
- Are there any problems with the kids?
- Is work preventing you from being with your family?

Year by year we explore questions like these together, and these interactions have enabled us to be more proactive in encouraging each other to create better marriage relationships.

Additionally, a few years ago we determined that we would like to spend more time together as families. Alison and I have subsequently invited the others to join us for holidays on a number of occasions. These vacations, in particular those with Carson and Brenda's family, have provided us with concentrated periods of togetherness that afford us unique opportunities to encourage one another. More importantly, perhaps, these occasions enable us to observe each other's family relationships up close. Such times are of inestimable value in providing us with the mutual insights and understanding that we need to support each other in nurturing and caring for our spouses.

To put it another way, we as covenant partners are not just available to help out in a crisis. Much more important is that we are committed to helping each other to excel in the day-to-day aspects of our marriages. Improving our marriages is an ongoing task, and the prodding, support, and advice of our friends can keep us properly focused on this all-important goal. Alison believes that my male friendships have been invaluable to our marriage. She says, "I know that your friends are not just concerned for your wellbeing but also for the health of our marriage. I am never threatened by your relationships with Carson and Bob because I know they will encourage you and hold you accountable in all your relationships."

Conclusion

Marriages are constantly under attack and difficult to sustain in today's society. Yet, given the support of friends, we can improve our chances of beating the odds and create successful and rewarding marriage unions. My covenant partners have helped me with my blind spots, provided me with a supportive environment to grow my marriage, and encouraged me in both crisis and routine to strive for excellence in my relationship with Alison.

Every marriage can benefit from this kind of support and encouragement. Are you willing to be a great husband? Why not take some time to think about whether or not your friends already encourage you in your marriage—or have the potential to do so? And why not talk to your wife about what kinds of things your friends can do to help you to become a better husband?

He who loves his wife, loves himself. . . . No one ever hated his own body, but he feeds and cares for it.
                                        —Ephesians 5:28b, 29

Chapter 13

Helping Me Love My Children

I'm sitting here in my study, staring at a stack of eighteen books that purport to hold the secret to being a better parent. They are all written by credible experts, and there is obviously no shortage of research to help us improve our parenting skills. Given this plethora of advice, how do we choose which theories to follow?

Alison and I have such diverse opinions on parenting that it has been hard to bring structure to our parenting efforts without bringing chaos into our marriage. As an example, I have always wanted to plan out and agree on a strategy for raising our kids. I am essentially future oriented and, therefore, thrive on brainstorming, dreaming, setting goals, and developing lists of what should be done. Give me a situation or a problem, and I'll develop a five-point plan to resolve it. In contrast, my wife Alison is much more of the moment. So while I am busy mulling over how important it is to spend time with our kids, she is actually doing it. While I am carefully contemplating which book our youngest daughter Stephanie should read, Alison will be sitting down with her reading a book.

Our styles may differ, but we are both committed to interact with our children on a meaningful level and to do what we can to contribute to their development into happy, secure, and well-adjusted adults. Therefore, we have agreed to a set of principles that we work toward as parents. These same principles are essentially common to Carson and Bob, and so our covenant becomes an important means of support in our efforts to make the best of our relationships with our children.

Over the years, we've focused on the following three principles to motivate, strengthen, and guide our children: 1) endeavor to live a life worth emulating; 2) correct and discipline them with love; and 3) affirm and encourage each child as a unique and special gift from God.

Live a Life Worth Emulating

Youth speaker Jerry Johnston says that modeling the behavior that you want your offspring to imitate is one of the most significant acts parents can undertake.[1] Of course, that is usually easier said than done. In fact, if we're honest with ourselves, most of us probably don't want our kids to imitate our behavior, and our natural inclination is to say, "Do what I say, not what I do." Although we may think this at some point, we also know that it really isn't a very effective parenting approach. In fact, it often only serves to make adults look like hypocrites, not models whose actions should be followed.

As a covenant group we not only encourage each other to live lives worthy of being emulated by our children, we are also each concerned that we model our lives well for the sake of each other's children. For example, Bob has been a factor in encouraging Carson's son, Jason, to identify his interest in the practice of law. To further stimulate this, Bob has invited Jason to visit his office on a number of occasions. Not only does this provide Jason with a view of Bob at work, and a view of Bob's work, but he also gets hands-on experience by occasionally helping out around the office.

As a parent, I know that I am not certain how to best model behaviors and that I may, at times, lack the courage to do so. That is when our covenant friendship and the cumulative wisdom of several parents can be particularly beneficial. In the following paragraphs, Bob tells in his own words the story of a unique opportunity to display courage and develop character with his son as he and Jordan undertook an epic journey on one of the most demanding hiking trails in North America:

Bob and Jordan's Great Adventure

Bob: Crashing cold water carved out the pool where my son and I, having doffed our sweat-soaked clothes, swam, and enjoyed the freedom and sunshine of the wilderness at Tsusiat Falls on the coast of British Columbia. I thought of Carson and David even then—realizing that I never would have made it to the West Coast

Trail to face the pounding surf of the Pacific Ocean were it not for their cheers and support.

This journey really began many months earlier when Carson, David, and I had shared the fears and the sense of importance that we all felt at the prospect of our eldest children becoming teenagers within the next few months. We were each eager to celebrate, share in the joy, and launch our eldest children into this new phase of their lives. But we also wondered how we could do this in such a way that our children would carry the experience into the turbulent years ahead and remember it as time of participating in a significant rite of passage with their fathers.

After much discussion, we determined to create some event or celebration that would reflect the character of each child and create an unforgettable memory. That's when someone suggested the West Coast Trail: seventy-two kilometers of wilderness and adventure that provided a stiff physical challenge to even the most-fit adults. The more information I gathered, the more excited I became at the prospect of taking my son on a trek that would push him to the edge of his strength and mental toughness.

As my anticipation grew, it became more difficult for my wife, Renae, to understand why the two oldest males in her family had to "risk their lives" to have an "adventure" together. Couldn't we just go on a camping trip somewhere close to home? She had plenty of support for her perspective—virtually everyone I had spoken with agreed that taking a not-so-big thirteen-year-old on a seven-day wilderness trek (if the weather cooperated) was something akin to foolishness.

As a husband and father, it was obviously time for a reality check. I was stubborn and optimistic enough to think that we could do it, but with all the negative comments, it seemed that I might be venturing into territory too wild without giving it adequate thought.

I shared my fears with David and Carson, explaining that I was afraid to risk making a wrong decision. After all, even the best advice confirmed that this was a dangerous trek and, frankly, I hadn't been camping since I was a teenager. I had been a Queen's Scout and trained in some wilderness survival back then, but it seemed like a lifetime ago, and I wondered if I could remember it if needed.

Our son Jordan was small for thirteen and had never been on an overnight camping trip. Neither had he ever carried a pack larger than his knapsack filled with books and lunch, nor walked farther than a day's scamper around Disneyland. But he also is an adventuresome sort with a vivid imagination, a lust for more thrills than he should experience, and a reluctance to admit fear. Even so, I knew that there would be times when the Trail demanded more than he was willing to give.

How would I react when he wanted to quit? Would that situation create more bad will than was worth risking? How would we get along when the drudgery of setting up camp, collecting firewood, cooking, cleaning up, and striking camp became evident? Would he hate the work so much that he would fail to enjoy the adventure? What if the weather made the journey even more difficult? What if Jordan got hurt, or worse? I began to wonder whether I was simply being a foolish romantic, who longed for a swashbuckling adventure.

Bob and Carson listened to all my doubts and questions. They asked hard questions and plumbed my reasons dispassionately. But the key questions they asked were, "Why do you want to do this?" and, "Is this trip for you or for Jordan?"

After probing my own motivation, I responded that, "I wanted to do something together that would live on as a vibrant memory of a time of adventure and achievement." Gaining this clarity about my motivation helped me to focus on my relationship with my son—not on the dangers of the trip. I now knew that I simply wanted to instill significance on an event that could only be done by accomplishing something that was seemingly beyond our reach. Carson's and David's questions then turned to support and encouragement, saying, "Then you should do it for the two of you."

So we did—and we not only survived, but God seemed to smile on our adventurous trek. Thanks to the encouragement of my friends, I was willing to take this risk. Without them, I would have certainly succumbed to saner reasoning and waited until Jordan was older and more experienced to take the trip.

But now the memories of this adventure will live on in my mind—and Jordan's—forever. I can see him telling his grandchildren about stepping on the burning coal and scalding his foot so badly he couldn't sleep, yet still trudging on the next day so that we could conquer the trail. Or how we slogged through mud bogs up to his waist and sidestepped along swinging rope bridges and slippery sandstone shelves, where one missed step would mean a fall of a hundred feet or more. Or even how we struggled with fully loaded packs to climb the sheer walls of creek canyons on two-by-four ladders several hundred feet in height with half-rotted rungs and not so much as a guardrail to cling to. I suspect that even the gray whales that fed on the ocean floor and spouted in the surf will, over time, become close enough to have touched. It was truly a father-son adventure of epic proportion. We had done it—together.

Had it not been for my partners at home, who could only enter into our joy by seeing the pictures and hearing the tales, this story might never have been written. Carson and David offered me two gifts: they got me thinking about the possibility of the trip and then gave me the clarity and courage to act.

This challenging hike enabled Jordan to learn to face some grueling adversity and not give up. The next time he is tempted to quit some grueling endeavor, he will surely draw on the memory of this success and, perhaps, keep going when he might not have done so otherwise. (As I write this he has just completed boot camp and has been invited to candidate for the prestigious Navy Seals!)

The character that we instill in our children "will chart a course . . . of happiness or despair, success or failure, and construction or destruction."[2] The challenge of conquering the West Coast Trail proved to be a real character-building experience for Jordan. But it doesn't always take an extreme hiking expedition to do so—any opportunity that we have to face and conquer challenges together with our children will help us to accomplish this.

So what are you doing to model character—and build character—in your children's lives?

Disciplining with Love

Each of us has experienced times where our kids have been in difficult situations and when being a parent hasn't been easy. At such times in my parenthood, it has been helpful to think of comments made by Zig Ziglar about disciplining our children in love. Ziglar is one of the most popular speakers in North America, and he writes about two important axioms: 1) "The child who has not been disciplined with love by his little world will be disciplined, generally without love, by the big world."[3] 2) "Real love demands that you do what is best for your child, not necessarily what your child wants you to do or what is easiest for you."[4]

Trouble in PUE-ville

Carson Pue is a great father. In fact, I think he is one of the best I know. But, like all of us, he's not perfect. Consider the following experience he and Brenda had with their eldest son. It was a major parenting crisis, and he describes the situation and the supportive roles that Bob and I played:

> *Carson:* I had already picked up the phone in my home office when my wife, Brenda, came to the door pleading, "Please don't call David or Bob!" Her face showed the mixture of fear and shame that is surely felt by all mothers of children who run away. "But Brenda, this is exactly when I should call Bob and David. This is what our covenant is all about." She continued to plead, "I don't want anyone to know that Jason has run away. Not yet." I put down the phone.
>
> I knew what she meant. It was awkward to share this with anyone—especially since we placed such high expectations on our parenting roles. The fact that I am a pastor, who bears all the usual expectations for raising perfect kids, didn't help. But as we discussed it, we both agreed that we were in over our heads. We needed the support of friends who wouldn't think any less of us but who would want to know so they could be there for us.
>
> Despite my experience as a youth pastor, tonight I had not done things right. It began simply enough—our son Jason had been grounded and his punishment included not being permitted to use the phone. But Brenda and I agreed that he could call back a neighbor who had asked him to baby-sit. So Jason left the room to make the call.
>
> I lost track of the time and later on picked up an extension phone to make a call—only to hear Jason talking to a friend! I immediately told him to hang up. But like a well-trained attorney, Jason told me that he had called a friend to "find out if there was a basketball practice on the day [he] was asked to baby-sit." He then stated, "You can call him if you don't believe me!"

Something didn't sit right with me. A heaviness in the pit of my stomach exacerbated my doubts that Jason was telling the truth. He had lied to us before and we had spent a great deal of time encouraging him to become more truthful, so I decided to challenge him. "Call your friend," I commanded, "I want to find out if you are telling the truth."

The rage was already beginning to build within me as Jason realized I was calling his bluff. He stared at the floor and mumbled, "It was not . . ."

There was more to that sentence, but to be honest I can't remember it. I lost it. I chased Jason upstairs to his room shouting, "You looked me right in the eyes and lied to me!" I pushed him onto his bed and uttered ridiculous phrases like, "You are grounded for life!" and, "Life as you've known it is over until after high school."

I can now laugh at the brilliant words that teenagers are capable of evoking from their parents at moments like that. But at the time, I was in a rage. I felt betrayed, unloved, despised, and deceived by my then thirteen-year-old son. I flopped onto my bed and sobbed. Brenda came in and held me. But while we talked, Jason quietly slipped out of the house and ran, we know now, until he arrived at the home of a friend, several miles from our home.

Brenda and I discovered he was gone when we went to his room to apologize and to suggest how we could work things out together. He was nowhere to be found. It was almost an hour and a half later when his friend's mother called to say that Jason was there, but he did not want to come home. We were relieved to know that Jason was safe but didn't know how to address this particular situation. We were haunted by the fact that he did not want to come home. I felt like the "father failure of the year" and used even stronger language to express this to Bob when I called to tell him that Jason had run away.

I could sense Bob's concern in the silence that followed. He listened carefully as I described how I had lost it when I caught Jason lying to me. As Bob listened, I could hear the heartbeat of both a friend and a father who would not abandon me. I also knew he loved my son and wanted the best for both of us. Without hesitation, Bob offered excellent counsel and was willing to come over and be with us. It was comforting, as Bob allowed me to confess my sense of failure and helped me to refocus on how to approach my now prodigal son.

The biblical story of the prodigal son took on new meaning for me that night. I became the father who waited outside my home, looking, searching, and yearning for my son to return. When Jason returned home early the next morning, I would have gladly killed the fatted calf and partied!

Looking back on the crisis, both of my covenant partners were there for me. Bob helped immediately through his level-headed thinking and with his intimate knowledge of Jason (who is similar to Bob in many ways). David complemented Bob's assistance by sharing in my brokenness. David is usually quick to try to fix things, but on this night he simply let me tell my story and reaffirmed his commitment to walk with me—not only through this night but all the nights that will follow with Jason, or my other sons, Jeremy and Jonathan.

David also followed up by calling Jason himself several days later. I am not sure what all was said in that phone call, but I suspect it was quite helpful since Jason now carries "Uncle Dave's" private phone number in his wallet. It was agreed that if Jason ever needed to get some space from mom or dad in the future, his Uncle Dave would come and get him from wherever he was and take him to the Bentall home.

We have crossed other lines with Jason since that night, but Brenda and I have since learned how to better communicate with our teenager. We have told him that kids don't come with an owner's manual, but we're trying our best. In many ways, the three of us (Dave, Bob, and I) also crossed a new line in our covenant relationship. I became acutely aware of the challenges still ahead in our role as parents and the need for covenant friends to carry us through.

Trouble at the Bentalls

When he was 18 years old, our son Jon was caught disobeying school rules while out of town at a hockey tournament. He and a friend also got in a little bit of trouble with the local police, and this resulted in some stern discipline from the headmaster. I was at a loss as to how to respond. On the one hand, I wanted to ensure that Jon had learned from the experience and knew that I was concerned about his behavior. On the other hand, I wanted him to know that I still loved him and wanted a close relationship with him. As a parent, what should I do?

Alison and I talked about grounding him or revoking his driving privileges. We pondered what kind of penance might be appropriate and even contemplated whether we would still let him live under our roof if things continued in the direction they were going. This was serious stuff for us. We knew that one false move might alienate us from our son, and we definitely didn't want to push him out onto the streets. However, we could not allow the current state of affairs to continue.

Carson and Bob each helped me to develop an action plan so that I could help Jon through that period of time. We decided on a period of grounding, but we allowed Jon's good behavior to be rewarded by shortening the grounding period. We dealt with the conditions that were necessary for Jon to still live in our home. It was a difficult time, yet I could be clear headed, loving, and firm all at the same time, in part, because of the support of my two friends.

Carson also offered to meet with Jon. I welcomed this, as I thought an independent party might, perhaps, help keep us from losing contact if things got worse. I knew Carson had previously been through a tough time with his son, and I hoped that he would be able to empathize with Jon in a way that I didn't think I could. Two years later when I asked Jon's permission to write about this incident, Jon told me to mention how helpful it had been for him to meet with Carson. He said, "I had lunch with Carson, and he helped me sort things out because he could see both sides. He was a parent who had a kid that was roughly my age, yet he had been a kid once too and understood what I was going through." What a gift to have someone who loved our son almost as much as we did and was willing to take the time to talk with him during a crisis.

Encourage Each Child
As a Special Gift from God

Each of us is a unique gift to the world, direct from the hand of God. As we come to understand this, we are able to develop a healthy self-concept and appropriate self-esteem. Both are integral to living a healthy life with significant relationships. As parents, we endeavor to foster this understanding in our children's lives through focusing on the good, playing with them, and setting goals.

Focus on the Good

Sometimes, as demonstrated above, the good qualities in our kids are overshadowed by the things they do while they are learning to individuate. That's when we need friends to help us to remember to focus on the good stuff. The night that Jason ran away, Carson needed emotional support, a sounding board, and an adult that his son could talk to when the communication lines were down. As covenant friends, we were able to offer these three gifts to him.

J. P. Getty, one of the twentieth century's most successful business leaders, was once asked how he was able to successfully manage the people who worked for him. (Amazingly, he had forty-two millionaires working for him at one time.) Getty said that he believed people were a lot like a gold mine—"there may be a lot of dirt, but you don't find the gold by focusing on the dirt."[5]

Similarly, as a covenant, we make it a point to stand with each other, to encourage each other to see the best in our kids and to remind each other to focus on the gold that is present in their lives (not the dirt).

Play with Them

Taking time to play with your children is an excellent means of developing their sense of value and self-worth. Again, it is one thing to agree with this and quite another to put it into practice. It often means that we have to set aside some of our own interests, including career, community activities, or hobbies. As a covenant group, we agree that this is an important part of being a parent and, therefore, we take time to routinely check that each one of us is doing this. We have further facilitated our opportunities to do this by taking vacations together and taking part in various sporting activities that enable us to hang out and play with each other's kids.

Set Goals

Alison and I have begun to take time to set goals with our children each year on their birthdays. In addition to a more traditional family celebration, we offer to take each child out for a special evening to talk more personally about physical, academic, financial, relational, and spiritual goals. So far, this has not revolutionized anyone of our kids' lives, but we are hoping to help them cultivate positive habits and outcomes by helping them to set goals on a regular basis.

Our covenant friendship has helped me to have a context for this exercise, because Carson and Bob both have children of similar ages. Consequently, they have assisted me in thinking more clearly what goals are appropriate for each of my children at their various age levels. I've also learned from each of my friends what processes they have used to set their personal and family goals.

Conclusion

Carson, Bob, and I all have high standards and, as a result, can easily be too demanding of our kids. Sharing with each other, in some detail, the trials and journeys of parenting has helped us all to be more realistic and effective in dealing with our children's various challenges.

Our children have certainly given us lots of joy, but there have also been lots of challenges. Unfortunately, because children do not come with parenting manuals, we have had almost all our training on the job. It has been terrific to have two other fathers to lean on as I have sought to become a parent. The close friendship we share has helped us all in striving to live lives worthy of emulation, in disciplining our kids with love, and in celebrating and affirming them in their uniqueness. I think all kids deserve to be parented in this way. To become effective parents, we need the support and encouragement of other like-minded parents who are willing to help us stay the course. I know I am a better parent because of my friendships, and if my children go on to be great adults who accomplish marvelous things, I won't mind sharing the credit one bit.

Listen my son, to your Father's instruction. . . .
Do not forsake your Mother's teaching.
They will be a garland to garner your head,
and a chain to adorn your neck.

—Proverbs 1:8, 9, NIV

Chapter 14

Helping Me in My Career

Ours is a world in which work has become dominant, and we identify ourselves in terms of what we do, not who our friends are.[1]

Sadly, the above statement is essentially true for most men in today's culture. "What do you do?" is undoubtedly the most commonly asked question when men first meet each other. Without even thinking about it, we define ourselves in terms of our careers. This is understandable, as most of us devote the majority of our waking hours to our work. However, we also have to remember that who we are is very different from what we do. And, if the truth were known, many of us would probably prefer to be known as something more than what we do.

Friends who know us well play a critical role in our lives by reminding us of the distinction between who we are and what we do. Their insight into our dreams, our longing for significance, and our desires for our families enable them to provide unique encouragement to us. They can keep us focused on pursuing our careers in a way that is consistent with our values, our priorities, and our faith. Moreover, they can prompt us and give us the added confidence and courage that we may need to take the bold steps (such as career change) that may be necessary to achieve what we have been created to do.

Friends don't need to have similar careers to offer this kind of assistance and support. Bob, Carson, and I couldn't have chosen more divergent career paths. In fact, it is the radical differences in our professions, combined with our different perspectives on life, that create the dynamic and insightful interactions that have motivated and assisted us so much in our respective careers. This support has proven to be particularly significant when we are in the midst of important career decisions or difficulties. In this chapter, we will explore some of the pivotal events that have shaped each of our careers. As we do this, you will see how our covenant friendship has enabled each of us to better manage our professional lives.

Carson's Career

Carson has a passion for people. He is an encourager at heart, and one who loves to enable and inspire personal growth in those around him. Consequently, he has been successful in his interactions with others when working in various people-oriented positions. He has worked in sales at Pue's Interior Furnishings, as a dean of residence in Calgary, and as an associate pastor at large churches in both downtown Calgary and Vancouver. Carson has always enjoyed quality relationships, so it should be no surprise that his friends have played an integral role in helping him through each of these career shifts.

Years ago, Carson became the Community Minister at First Baptist Church in Vancouver. Because Bob served there as a deacon, he had some formal contact with Carson but, over a period of time, their interactions became more personal.

After a few years at the church, Carson realized that he was ready for a change in his career. Although he felt called to full-time ministry, he was not certain that First Baptist Church was still the best place for him to fulfill that calling. As his connection with Bob grew more personal, he communicated this concern to him.

Coincidentally, at that time, Bob was also chairman of the board for Insight for Living Ministries in Canada. This was the international radio ministry associated with Chuck Swindoll, and its leadership just happened to be looking for a new Canadian executive director. Bob's wife, Renae, was the first to suggest that the ministry explore the possibility of Carson taking on the job. It turned out to be a good match, and through this new opportunity Carson was better able to utilize his gifts and strengths as he became a pastor to pastors. As a result, Bob and Carson became collaborators on strategic and leadership issues, and they were collectively able to shape and implement a successful plan for growth at Insight for Living Ministries in Canada.

After five fulfilling years at Insight for Living, Carson was invited to move to North Carolina to become the international president of Arrow Leadership, an organization that identifies and trains future leaders for ministry. With affiliates in seven countries around the world, it is a highly-regarded international training enterprise. Carson himself is a graduate and, along with his wife Brenda, was instrumental in organizing the first Canadian classes.

His previous association with the ministry was one of the factors that drew him to the opportunity. But there were some drawbacks. His family was deeply rooted in the community of Langley, British Columbia; his eldest son would be graduating in less than two years; his other boys were in the critical teen and preteen years, and moving at this stage could prove difficult for them. In addition, Carson also felt that our covenant friendship was something that he wanted to maintain from close range rather than from halfway across the continent.

I thought these reasons were legitimate, but I also believed that he would make a great leader for this ministry. We began to discuss whether there might be another way to make this work.

In what proved to be a pivotal conversation, I asked Carson whether he might propose that Arrow move its international headquarters to Langley. Given today's technology and the ease of modern travel, I argued that its leadership training could be accomplished (and located) virtually anywhere. After some reflection and prayer, Carson proposed this to the board of Arrow Leadership and, much to his surprise and delight, they agreed. The headquarters was subsequently moved to Canada, and Carson became the new president of Arrow Leadership Ministries.

Initially, it was thought that there might be some formal association with Insight for Living, and so Bob, who was still connected to that organization, was chosen to act as the interim Chair of Arrow Leadership. He served in this capacity for two years, until the demands of his law practice became overwhelming. Bob then asked me to assume the chair at the end of his term. I firmly supported the work of Arrow and was already a donor to the ministry. But I would be less than honest if I didn't confess that I agreed to take on the chairman's role, in part, as a favor to Bob and to Carson. As I mentioned in chapter 7, I eventually withdrew from this role. The point is that through these various roles, both Bob and I were able to assist Carson in his ministry—and to support him as he chose to take bold steps in his career.

How all this came together seems rather miraculous, and it hasn't always been easy. Over the past several years, Carson has had numerous challenges at Arrow. There have been tough issues related to strategic planning, staffing, and fundraising. Even though I am no longer the board chair, these are areas where I have had considerable experience, and I have been able to offer the benefit of my background to Carson as he continues to develop this exciting ministry.

David's Career

For more than twenty years, Bob has played an integral role in my life as a professional advisor. In fact, my professional relationship with Bob predates our covenant, as I explained in chapter 3. This combination of being both a friend and advisor is increasingly common, as evidenced by the growing popularity of business mentoring programs. Those of you who have had the privilege of working professionally with friends will surely appreciate the added dimension and enriched interaction that this can bring to a work environment. Granted, the occasional problem can crop up, but it is obviously preferable to work with and be advised by people whose companionship we enjoy and who genuinely want the best for us.

Our relationship is, perhaps, more unusual in that Bob and I tend to function like mutual mentors. We have both had the privilege of being mentored by older men and the responsibility of mentoring younger ones. These experiences have enriched our lives and better enabled us to achieve success in the business world.

Some of the following points have already been briefly mentioned, but it's worthwhile to note the full spectrum of contributions that Bob has made to me throughout my career. In particular, Bob has:

- Helped me to carry the emotional load of my work. Bob has helped me to think through career problems and decisions, particularly as I poured out my thoughts when we trained together for triathlons. He listened to me as we plodded around the track—and it was a gift of immeasurable value since I am primarily an auditory learner. These conversations helped me to unburden my soul, and Bob's capacity to listen to me and support me functioned to lighten my load considerably.

- Provided advice in making decisions. There is an old saying in business that asserts, "It's lonely at the top." It's true, and most people who rise to leadership positions in their careers eventually discover this. For example, whom can you trust to discuss hiring or firing decisions? Or debate the wisdom of selling shares or the threat of legal action? Certainly, there are professional consultants and colleagues for these purposes, but the advice of a friend who knows every aspect of your life produces an element of trust that isn't typically found with paid consultants.

- Consistently asked the tough questions. Bob has both the insight and courage to pose good questions, as evidenced when I debated selling my shares in our family business. He simply asked, "If someone offered to sell you a construction company, would you buy it?" I readily answered that I wouldn't—because I had no real passion for the construction business.

  That one question brought me to realize that I was not well suited to run a construction company. Consequently, it encouraged me to make a career (and life) changing decision to sell our family construction business.

- Provided a comprehensive view of my life—not just my career. Just yesterday, a lawyer told me, "When you are in need of help or support, you may not have the time or ability to articulate the whole story." In other words, if you wait until a crisis strikes before you initiate a relationship with a professional advisor, it may be too late. Even the most capable advisors might not have the time to learn all the implications of a situation if they don't really know you. Under such circumstances, their advice may be limited in its effectiveness. On the other hand, when a client and advisor have a long-standing relationship, it is far more likely that the client will obtain advice that takes all of the nuances of important issues into account—even in the midst of a crisis.

So it is in my relationship with Bob. His knowledge of me goes beyond the professional details, and therefore his advice to me is, quite literally, priceless. He knows my strengths and weaknesses, as well as my hopes and dreams. His knowledge of me—and my life—has enabled him to help me in my career in a way that few others could have.

Bob's Career

When Bob turned thirty-nine, he wrote a sobering, reflective article that began with the simple words, "I'm thirty-nine." He posed and sought to answer such questions as, What have I done with my life so far? Where am I going on this journey? What is my vision, and what am I going to accomplish with my life? Faced with the reality of growing older, Bob wasn't sure that he was measuring up to his own expectations. He had a good education, a good career, and a growing family, but was he making any real difference in the world?

Bob had worked for more than two decades with major law firms in downtown Vancouver. He had also discovered that the harder he worked, the more work he had to do. Meanwhile, he had a wife and three children. As life flew by, Bob realized that there were too many days when time with his family simply didn't happen. What difference was he making with all of his efforts in the office? His clients were satisfied, but what about those he loved? What about his own sense of satisfaction? Was he achieving what he really wanted—or was he merely caught on the same workaholic treadmill as so many others?

As a result of this time of contemplation, Bob made a decision to move his law practice out of the downtown, where he had been a partner with a major international firm. He resolved that moving to a rural environment would offer him the opportunity to lead a more balanced lifestyle, to solidify his relationship with his wife, and to establish a better pattern of living for his entire family. Bob wasn't going to give up the practice of law, but he was going to try to work in such a way that his family would see more of him and he more of them.

In essence, he told his family that he recognized they had been getting short shrift and he wanted to do what was necessary to create more balance in their lives. As a result, Bob joined Baker Newby, a leading firm in the Fraser Valley, just fifty miles east of Vancouver. At the same time, he purchased a small acreage backing onto a creek and constructed a dream home with his wife, Renae.

A few years later, Bob took another bold step and started his own law firm. The business has done well from the start, but making the decision to invest a large portion of their life savings and to borrow the working capital necessary to establish a new enterprise was not easy. After all, Bob had worked for major firms for more than twenty years, and the prospects of cutting the umbilical cord were somewhat frightening. But as Bob launched his dream, he gained courage from the love and support of two friends who would be there for him in difficult times.

Carson and I didn't make Bob's decision for him. But Bob was better able to make the decision because, in the context of our friendship, he had been consistently talking about his life, his vision, his family, and his work with two friends who cared enough to encourage him to make the changes that he needed to find fulfillment.

The Harvard Boys

Our covenant friendship is not unique. There are a number of other men who have developed relationships that similarly span career, family, and personal interests. More than ten years ago, Kevin Jenkins, a successful businessman and former president of Canadian Airlines, met three other executives while attending the Harvard Business School. During their two-year tenure in Boston, they attended a regular Bible study together and developed a close relationship. Since then they have faithfully and purposefully maintained this relationship over distance, time, and various endeavors. Kevin and I are good friends, and over the years we have discussed the benefits and significance of close friendships to our lives and careers.

Kevin considers his friendship with "the Harvard boys" as a community that isn't just there for advice or accountability. Rather, his group reflects the idea of community espoused by Henri Nouwen, a scholar, gifted author, and priest. Nouwen believed that community is a safe place to forgive one another "for not being God and to celebrate each others' lives."

Within the safety of this community of friends, Kevin says, "We are transparent with each other—I know everything about them and they know everything about me. They know all the sins that I have identified in myself—pride, greed, lust, my shortcomings as a husband and father, etc. I know all the sins that they have identified in themselves. (Usually these are opportunities for prayer, not advice.) But the most important thing to me is that even though we know each other's faults in a way that few people know another person except their spouse, we love each other deeply. We would do anything for one another. We feel responsible for the success of each other's marriages. We are able to regularly pray informed prayers for each person and for the members of each other's families. We are committed to life-long friendship. We laugh and play together. It is the rarest of friendships—to be fully known and still fully loved!"

Clearly, he has found what I have found—that the company we keep has the potential to help us become better men, husbands, and fathers. It is not a new idea, but it is profound. C. S. Lewis writes about the powerful effect that men can have on one another and states that friendship "makes good men better and bad men worse."[2]

As the former head of a major international corporation, Kevin knows all too well the challenges of corporate leadership." He was CEO of Canadian Airlines when it was bought by Air Canada. It wasn't an easy time. He says, "Regardless of the inward doubts a leader may be having, he must outwardly convey vision, confidence, and a sense of hope. The most difficult time of my career was my last few months as CEO of Canadian

Airlines," yet it is in troubled times that the gift of friendship steps to the forefront. According to Kevin, "It was wonderful to have a confidential forum in which I could express my frustrations and challenges. I was free to express my true feelings to a group of men who loved me and were 'for' me whether I had a fancy business card or no business card at all."

Confidentiality is once again a key to the success of friendship—not just for sharing family and marital issues, but also for our careers. You could imagine the newspaper headlines if it were publicly known that CEO Kevin Jenkins had frustrations and doubts as he led an international airline. Yet, even when public knowledge of his concerns could have translated into major damage to the airline, Kevin had no qualms in talking openly with his friends. We can't ever underestimate the value of such unwavering confidence in confidants to a man who is at the top of his profession and otherwise would be, quite literally, alone with his thoughts.

Conclusion

We spend the majority of our waking hours pursuing our careers, and sometimes this leads us to think that our work defines who we are and is the only—or the most important—aspect of our lives. As C. S. Lewis said, if ambition is the desire to get ahead of others, then it is bad. But if it's the desire to "want to do a good thing well, then it is good."[3] Carson, Bob, and I are three men who are driven to be our best; we strive to do good things and to do them well. But even in working for good, we sometimes lose sight of the fact that who we are in this life is more than what we do.

The simple process of growing older can take its toll on a man and affect his sense of self-worth and accomplishment. Similarly, the process of changing jobs and adjusting to new professional circumstances can be very destabilizing and challenging. Even the reality of having to sell a business and/or radically alter one's life direction in midcareer can be almost impossible to face—by ourselves.

In all of the above, we need each other to pull us aside and speak the truth to us about our careers. Through the eyes of our friends, we can see our careers more clearly, and we are rightly reminded of our own worth at those times when we don't feel successful in our work. Kevin's experiences also make it clear that "the Harvard boys" lend this kind of support to each other and, thankfully, so do Carson, Bob, and I.

Friendship also provides the opportunity for each of us to offer our individual expertise to one another. As a result of our covenant, we now have a pastor who has more legal and business savvy than he might otherwise have had; a lawyer who is more marketing oriented, possessing a caring approach to people; and a businessman who is more sensitive to others and more legally astute than he might otherwise have been.

The sluggard craves and gets nothing,
But the desires of the diligent are fully satisfied.
—Proverbs 13:4, NIV

Chapter 15

Helping Me Get Fit

Several years ago, I was working out at a gym in Palm Springs, California, when I noticed two men who were obviously serious about weightlifting. One encouraged his training partner as he lifted the entire stack of weights on a universal gym biceps machine. The two men then traded places and, to my amazement, the first partner (about 250 pounds) stood on the weight machine while the second partner effortlessly lifted the entire stack of weights, plus the weight of his training partner!

Suddenly, my own efforts seemed rather paltry in comparison. Given that I have never been one to pass up an opportunity, I was determined to know what drove this real-life "Terminator." Propelled by curiosity, I approached and attempted to be nonchalant as I inquired how often he worked out. He explained that he was at the gym every day, eight hours a day, and that this regime was productive because he was able to isolate different muscle groups for each workout. Upon further probing, I discovered that just a few years earlier he had won the Mr. Universe title. Over the next week, we ran into each other several more times at the gym, and I found myself even more impressed by this man as he shared his life story with me. He had given up participating in competitions because he had come to understand that his drive to succeed as a bodybuilder had been fueled largely by pride and a desire to make himself look better than anyone else. He said that he would look in the mirror and worship his own physique. He now realized that this attitude, both self-centered and narcissistic, was not what God had intended for him.

In contrast, he now trains so that he can stay fit and act as a role model for kids. By doing demonstrations in prisons and high schools, he encourages young people to take care of their bodies and to think about life in all of its dimensions, including the spiritual. In other words, he now used his bodybuilding to glorify God and to help others rather than as a means to fuel self-worship. Here was a man who was transformed not only by fitness but also by God. It was a privilege to meet him.

Contemporary Problems

Movies that feature men like Arnold Schwarzenegger or Jackie Chan have given us an opportunity to observe the outstanding shape and physical feats that the human body can achieve. Magazines like *Men's Fitness* and *Muscle Mag* show us how we can supposedly attain a well-oiled, perfectly sculpted physique—usually in just a few short months! With promises like that, it is no wonder we have a culture that is increasingly obsessed with body shape. However, by observing a well-built body we can easily fall into envy, jealousy, or—if it's our own body—pride.

This obsession with the human physique is especially prevalent among young people. At school, the jocks and the beauty queens are somehow regarded as more worthy or more popular than the guy on the debating team or the head of the chess club. Young women frantically attempt to create bodies like those of the models they see in popular magazines. Men are jogging, dieting, weightlifting, and even taking unproved supplements in attempt to attain the youthful physique that Hollywood portrays.

Obviously, there is something wrong here. Fitness should be about more than just body shape. Can't there be motivators or goals for fitness other than attempting to create an object we like to look at in the mirror, or creating a body that will stroke our own egos or catch the attention of the opposite sex? A radically different reason to go for a run or to the gym, in addition to respecting our health, could be found in the opportunity of spending time with a friend. Most of us would consider calling a friend for a round of golf or a game of tennis. But friendship doesn't have to end—or start—with the game. These same friends can be the key to getting physically fit.

Fitness and Our Covenant

In our friendship covenant we have each naturally taken on leadership roles that correspond with our gifts, talents, and interests. Carson, the pastor, is our primary guide in spiritual matters. Similarly, Bob, an accomplished lawyer, has a very sharp mind and is probably the most level-headed and perceptive. That leaves me to give leadership in the area of fitness and physical health. Having enjoyed athletics throughout my life and having had the privilege of playing on two championship rugby teams, I don't mind giving the benefit of my experience to my friends—even though Carson and Bob don't exactly line up at my door to ask me for advice. However, it is probably accurate to say that our covenant was born through fitness activities.

My friendship with Bob first began to grow when he and I decided to improve our fitness by training for a twenty-four-hour fund-raising relay race. Our first day in training for this was quite unremarkable. We were only able to run about a mile before collapsing in exhaustion. We thought we were going to die. But that was January, and by the time the June relay arrived, we were each able to run 2.5 miles four times during a twenty-four hour period. We were so elated, you would think we had conquered Mount Everest.

My doctor then encouraged us to run farther. He pointed out that we were doing all the hard work (i.e., the first twenty minutes) without obtaining the benefit of the fat burning that comes from running for a longer period of time. Worse than that, we were missing out on the endorphin boost that comes after running for thirty or forty minutes. He suggested that we develop the capacity to run at least five miles. At first, Bob and I thought this was utterly impossible.

Giving in to his advice, we began to increase our distance bit by bit each week until we were finally running five miles for the very first time. It was a huge milestone and, feeling particularly triumphant, I then announced to Bob that I wanted to try a triathlon the next year. He thought this was insane but, being the good listener that he is, he didn't immediately say so out loud. (I think he inwardly assumed that I'd eventually give up on the idea.) Nevertheless, we worked toward this goal and completed a triathlon the following June. Together we have now run ten short-course triathlons.

When I was younger, I maintained a pretty good level of fitness while playing basketball and rugby throughout high school and then with varsity rugby at the University of British Columbia. Similarly, Bob was a college volleyball player and an active sportsman throughout university. However, the challenge of the law profession had shackled him to a desk for almost ten years. With the camaraderie, motivation, and discipline of running together and doing triathlons, we have both now achieved a better level of overall fitness than ever before in our lives.

Carson missed out on the triathlon journey, although I suspect that had we given him the choice, he would have declined to participate anyway. In fairness, I think it's easiest to describe Carson as the one in our group who would least likely be mistaken for a beanpole. But he reads more books in a year than I read in five or ten years! As we compared notes, we realized that the time I spend in athletics is the time that he spends nourishing his mind and spirit through literature. Nonetheless, Bob and I challenged Carson to begin to walk regularly and, with the aid of a portable radio and a dog that needed daily exercise, Carson launched a new phase in his life—exercise. He subsequently invested in a treadmill, and it has given him both the opportunity to read and sweat at the same time. As a result of our encouragement, Carson is now working to attain a higher level of fitness and, at the time of writing this book, Carson has lost more than forty pounds through a sustained diet and fitness program.

What Can Friends Do for One Another in Terms of Fitness?

In terms of fitness, we can first be an example for each other. Dave Whyte, who won British Columbia's High School Athlete of the Year award twice, was one of my best friends in high school. He set a great example for me during my teen years, and I am now trying to set a similar example for my friends and family in terms of demonstrating healthy eating habits and good fitness routines.

Second, we can be together in our athletic endeavors. Bob and I ran triathlons together for several years; more importantly, we trained together for them. Looking back, the events themselves weren't all that thrilling or rewarding, but our training journey (running together, talking together, breakfasting together, and even anticipating being together) is what has made the whole experience memorable, meaningful and, at times, fun. Like the business friendship mentioned in chapter 2, fitness can be a natural starting point for guys to get together. Deeper friendship can then develop over time and a shared interest.

Third, we can be an encouragement. When we are training or pursuing athletic goals, we often get discouraged. Results come more slowly than we think they should and, from time to time, we fail to meet our goals. During these times, friends stand with us and encourage us to carry on. There is no question that both Bob and I would have discontinued training for triathlons without each other's motivation and encouragement.

Fourth, we can help keep each other accountable to meet our goals. All of us find that time pressures and responsibilities make it hard to stay with our fitness routines. This may be why professional personal trainers have become so popular. They bring accountability and discipline to our fitness routines, even if we have to pay for it. Friends can do this for each other by exercising or training together, and it doesn't cost a thing—plus the accountability factor is almost as high as with a professional trainer.

At the time of this writing, Bob has recently experienced what he calls a breakthrough in his fitness regime. He has lost twenty-five unwanted pounds over several months, mostly as a result of his five workouts per week. He says he is feeling fitter than he has in decades. Each of us has utilized different approaches to achieving our goals, and in these past few years we have trained independently. However, no one could accurately say that we haven't been in this together.

Conclusion

Internal motivation is probably the weakest link in anyone's exercise regime. Dr. Kenneth Cooper, the American fitness guru and "father of aerobics," says, "One of the best ways to develop an inner drive to exercise regularly is to arrange to work out with a compatible companion or a group."[1] Our schedules will never magically open up and create a block of time that is convenient for a workout. Instead, the onus is on you to decide that you want to be healthy. "That means making a firm commitment that you will get off your backside and launch yourself on a life-changing program . . . that will give you more energy."[2]

Developing a good-looking body doesn't have to be the goal of fitness. Enhanced physical health is a natural byproduct of any training program, but men can gain further dividends by using workouts to develop friendships and, conversely, using friendships to improve their fitness. Friends who care about our health and our long-term wellness can encourage us, motivate us, and hold us accountable in our fitness programs.

So why not grab a friend, set some athletic goals, and start to build and strengthen the physical and relational dimensions of your life? You will not only transform your physical body, but you will also take a step forward in developing a transformational friendship.

Do you not know—your body is the dwelling place of God's spirit?

—1 Corinthians 6:19

You are beautifully and wonderfully made.

—Psalm 139:14a

Chapter 16

Helping Me Develop My Mind

Relationships have a significant influence on how—and what—we think. After all, it is the people that we spend time with who have the greatest impact on what kinds of things we are thinking about. This, in turn, influences our thought patterns and ultimately shapes our actions and our character. So perhaps it's time we all considered the impact that our friends have on our thinking. Do they have a positive or negative effect on your thoughts and actions?

The idea that our friends influence how we think and act is hardly new. As we were growing up, most of us were probably encouraged to choose our friends wisely. My dad often reminded me of the adage you can judge a man by his friends. The implication was that if I chose good friends, I would strive to become like them, but if I chose less desirable friends, I would become like them. Either way, he knew my friends would affect the kind of person I would ultimately become.

I am now convinced that my dad was right. Our thoughts and actions typically do mimic those of our peers. If our friends focus on the positive things in life, then it's highly likely that we will too. Much of this is subliminal. However, at a more conscious level, friends may also notice our habitual thinking patterns. When they do, they can assist us in filtering, or even changing our thought patterns. Just as a personal trainer can help us with our physical fitness, friends can encourage our mental fitness.

The rest of this chapter outlines some ways in which friends can help us to develop different thinking patterns.

Friends Can Help Us Think Clearly

Sometimes our patterns of thinking are so deeply engrained that we are not even aware of them or how strongly they influence our behavior. We may have developed negative or destructive patterns of thinking when we were young. As we age, they grow to be such an intrinsic part of our being that they almost become hardwired and begin to drive us, for good or ill. From time to time, we need someone to intervene, to help us to identify and help us evaluate our mind-sets, especially if we have developed some bad wiring.

For much of my life, I believed that my opinion was not valuable. This was perhaps influenced by the fact that my dad was a successful business executive who didn't often want—or ask for—my opinion. My dad believed in me and was my greatest fan, but in spite of this, he was perhaps more inclined to point out how or why he thought my thinking was wrong than to solicit my ideas.

The message that my opinion was not valued was further reinforced early in my career when I found myself in an environment where new ideas were not welcomed—and, in fact, were stifled. As a young executive, I was not encouraged to make decisions. A senior executive even told on one occasion, "I know you are smarter than me, David, but we are doing it my way." No wonder I had so little confidence in my own opinions.

Thankfully, over the years, Carson has identified my insecurity, this pattern of thinking, and is helping me to change. Through his efforts, he has helped me to overcome the tendency to believe that my ideas aren't good enough and has prompted me to stop hiding behind other people's opinions, especially those of experts.

The latter was a coping mechanism that I developed early in my career. While working at the Cadillac Fairview Corporation, I learned to quote senior colleagues to justify or support my decisions. At the time, I had almost no experience in making project-related decisions and, despite this, I was made responsible for a major shopping center redevelopment. With a $70-million expansion project on my plate at the age of twenty-nine, it isn't hard to imagine how nervous I was about making a wrong move. I began to compensate for my insecurity by not making any decisions until I could find a vice president who would endorse each particular suggestion. Since the corporation had a vice president in charge of almost every conceivable aspect of a project (architecture, leasing, finance, management, legal, development, and construction), this strategy worked like a charm. Unfortunately, it also meant that I was constantly suborning my decision-making to the input of others.

Years later, I could still be found avoiding taking ownership for my opinions. Carson noticed this when a friend challenged me to seek forgiveness from a member of our extended family. There had been a break in the relationship for more than ten years, and previous attempts to reestablish dialogue had failed. So I decided to take on the challenge and, as a result, that relationship was put on a better footing.

But as I talked to Carson about this, he noted that I referred to my efforts to improve this relationship as though they were entirely someone else's doing. To be fair, my friend is the one who first challenged or encouraged me to act. Yet, ultimately, I was the one who determined I wanted to be reconciled, and I was the one who sought the reconciliation by seeking forgiveness. That is, the choice for reconciliation was mine, even though my actions were stimulated by someone else's encouragement and suggestion.

Carson also noted that I tend to quote the advice of other coaches when offering tips to water-skiers. For instance, instead of saying, "I think it might help if you hold onto the handle until you are wide of the buoy line," I would be more apt to say, "When I was coached by the USA team coach last summer, he told me to try this." Even though I had become an experienced tournament water-skier, I would still defer to someone else's judgment when coaching others. Even more astonishing is that I wasn't even aware that I was doing so!

Ever since Carson pointed out this pattern of thinking, I have focused on developing a new pattern of expressing my thoughts. The key that unlocked the door to this change was that my friend helped be to recognize that my opinions had value and he gave me confidence to begin voicing them.

Friends Can Help Us to Think More Positively of Others

Although most of us enjoy the stimulation of good conversation with friends, too much of our everyday talk is superficial and of little consequence. What is worse, it is all too easy for shallow conversations by the watercooler or over a beer to deteriorate into criticism, gossip, or complaints. Most of us have heard the expression that, unbridled, "the tongue can kill," and yet how often do we pause to consider the potential injury of the gossip we share with friends? Moreover, how many of us look to our friends to help us avoid these natural inclinations and instead inspire us to be less critical and judgmental?

In my experience, it was a dear, little old lady I met in Palm Springs who best modeled for me the power of speaking positively, even when criticism might have be justified. For more than forty years, she and her husband had lived on the ranch where our family annually vacationed. Over afternoon tea, I remember telling her that I really liked the new general manager and asked her what she thought of him. Without any negative comment, she simply changed the subject and told me how much she liked the changes that had been made to the roads on the property. In one deft move—and without saying a critical word—she had intimated that she was not enamored of the general manager, yet had not stooped to criticize. She took the "high road" by avoiding any negative inference. I was amazed and inspired by her approach.

I am very fortunate to have Carson and Bob, two friends who, like that lady, remind me to avoid being critical of others. More importantly, when the three of us are together, we try to avoid anything that would remotely resemble a gossip session. It would be easy to talk about others but, in contrast, we try to speak to each other and about others in ways that will "be good and helpful, so that our words will be an encouragement to those who hear them" (Ephesians 4:29). Given that we live in a culture that seems more directed toward sarcasm and criticism, this is not always easy. We can choose, however, to make positive contributions—with the support and help of our friends.

Friends Can Encourage One Another to Grow Intellectually

Lifelong learning is now accepted as normal and necessary if an individual wants to remain employed or employable. Society's rapid pace of change, accelerated by new technologies, has made it essential for each of us to engage in a process of ongoing education and self-development. In most cases however, unless our study involves a formal academic environment or some type of seminar, our efforts can be a solitary exercise.

Carson, Bob, and I are involved in stimulating one another's intellectual growth. One example of this is our gathering together for mutual study. When our covenant group recognized the need to learn how to be better parents, we committed ourselves to monthly meetings, together with our wives, to view and discuss a videotape series on parenting. We learned a great deal from these discussions, yet it is something that each of us would not likely have taken time for on our own.

Looking at intellectual development from another angle, Carson has shown me that reading is a discipline that I need to practice to a greater extent. I had always assumed that this world was made up of readers and nonreaders and that I fell into the latter category. But Carson, who is a voracious reader, has demonstrated to me that reading is a matter of priorities, discipline, and habit. I don't use the word *discipline* lightly; I truly believe that we need to discipline our minds to read. We are constantly presented with choices about how we spend our time—and we may sometimes find it much easier to just flop down on the couch and watch television.

Thus I have come to realize that through discipline I can become a better reader. Just as I have encouraged Carson to replace some of his reading time with fitness, so he has encouraged me to replace some of my fitness time with reading. My dad was a great reader, and while I was always amazed at how much he would read, I now see how this discipline kept him well informed, inspired his career, and assisted him in being a great conversationalist.

It has been said that "you will be the same person you are today except for the books you read and the people you meet."[1] Books influence our thinking by offering us new ideas and perspectives, while challenging our own. Bit by bit and book by book, our minds are stretched.

Friends Can Teach Us How to Reflect

Bobb Beihl, president of the Masterplanning Group and a management consultant to corporate leaders, states, "Wisdom comes from putting time between opportunity and decision." For example, if you see an ad for a car that catches your eye, it might be foolish to run out and buy it immediately. However, should you take the time to test drive it, compare it with the alternatives, and review its price in relation to your budget, it may well be the wise choice. Obviously, there are times when we need to act quickly, but taking time to reflect on a decision before we act is more typically the best course of action.

This advice does not only apply to specific decisions. We will live more wisely, in a general sense, if we periodically invest time to reflect on what our priorities are and what they should be. Hence, it makes sense to build time to withdraw into our regular routine and, on occasion, to take a significant block of time to consider, at a deeper level, what is happening in on our lives. Having taken time to reflect, we can then reenter the flow of life more prepared to live the lives we want.

Whenever Bob, Carson, and I meet, we usually take time to reflect and report to each other about how things are going in our lives, including both our successes and our failures. This process forces us to look back at what we have accomplished and stimulates us to think about what lies ahead. We can assess our priorities more accurately and then determine what we need to do to keep our lives moving in the direction we desire.

This kind of reflection can happen effectively on an individual level, in the context of a business affinity group or a sports team, or as part of a church group. I have had the benefit of each of these. Yet, none can compare to the depth and substance I have encountered by reflecting on my life in the company of my two closest friends, those who know me inside out and who are committed to supporting me for the rest of my life.

Quiet Meditation Can Be Life-Affirming

The word *meditation* has several different connotations and is often equated with eastern religions or monastic mystics. A helpful notion for me has been to compare meditation to a cow chewing its cud. After swallowing its food, a cow will then regurgitate it and chew it again to obtain more nutrients. Similarly, if we focus on truth or memorized information, we can retrieve them from memory and mull them over in our minds, chewing on their meaning and continuing to extract their significance to us. You may note that this kind of meditation is in stark contrast to the more common type of meditation that inclines people to empty their minds and to focus inwardly or to focus on a single word or idea.

I am convinced that if we meditate on or contemplate things that are worthy, we can transform our minds by filling them with positive, life-changing truth. Thus, the truth that is found in the Bible provides ideal food for meditation, as it helps us to continually focus our minds on the very thoughts of God.

I am the first to admit that meditation doesn't come naturally or easily to me. As I mentioned in an earlier chapter, our covenant group has frequently gone for short retreats to Westminster Abbey, a Benedictine monastery located just outside of Vancouver. In this context, I have had to learn to spend time in solitude, quietly studying my Bible and meditating on its truths. I had no idea how motivating and life affirming such an experience could be! Just as a shower invigorates the body, I have found that times of solitude can rejuvenate the mind.

Bob thrives in this environment, and in the paragraphs below he takes you into this unique setting that has meant so much to our group.

Bob: In a world that rushes to get to tomorrow, the idea of a retreat often seems counterproductive. But it has been in retreat, at the Abbey, that we have been free to wander in ways our intellects could not do in our normal lives. The Abbey bristles in intelligence and education, and it provides a perfect setting to engage in and focus on unhurried exploration of thoughts, feelings, and plans that would otherwise get lost in the daily press of living. The concerns of the world we live in and the frantic pace we keep depart from our minds as we take in the one-hundred-eighty degree view of the Fraser River, the Coast Mountains, the fertile farmlands, and even some of the burgeoning cities.

It is here that we have seen how a community, with a covenant that is deeper and more mystical than our own, functions. While sharing silent meals with the Benedictine monks, we have learned that words are not necessary to communicate commitment or ideas. Our covenant friendship has benefited from experiencing their values and simplicity as they have extended hospitality to us as members of their extended family.

Our Friends Can Support Us in Our Dreams

What do you hope to achieve with your life? What do you want your future to look like? Do you long for a happier, closer family life? Do you want to achieve something memorable with your career? What are your dreams? More importantly, are they being nourished by others?

Everything we achieve begins with a thought or an idea that, when developed, may give birth to a dream or a vision. If our thoughts are the seeds of our dreams, then it is imperative that we think well and perceptively. However, having brilliant thoughts and dreams for positive change isn't enough in and of itself. We must also *act* on our dreams, and that is when we often encounter obstacles. One way to get help in overcoming the inevitable hurdles is to cultivate friendships with those who will actively support our dreams. The advice or words of a friend can be the fuel that is necessary for you to carry on in the face of adversity and regain your footing when you stumble.

In his autobiography, billionaire Jimmy Pattison, British Columbia's most successful entrepreneur, reflects on the significance of our dreams and poignantly states that if we have the ability to dream, then we also have the ability to achieve that dream.[2] Although this may not always hold true for all, it's an inspiring concept that can motivate us to actively work to fulfill our dreams.

Unfortunately, by the time we reach adulthood, many of us have had our dreams crushed or trampled underfoot. Our teachers and our parents have overwhelmed us with the imperative to be realistic in looking to the future. As a result, we have been utterly discouraged from dreaming and may not even feel safe in confessing our dreams to others without fear of ridicule. In sharp contrast, our covenant group provides a safe environment for us to actively encourage one another to dream, to share our dreams and to take steps to pursue those dreams. As a result of their support, I have been encouraged to pursue two of my lifelong dreams—to win a national waterskiing championship and to write a book (this one). Similarly, with our support, Bob had the courage to achieve his dream of starting his own law firm, and Carson had the confidence to propose that the international headquarters for Arrow Leadership be moved to his community so he could accept the invitation to be its leader. Without the mutual support of covenant friendship, we might have missed these life-affirming opportunities to pursue our dreams.

Conclusion

If you want to develop your intellect, it is probably a good idea to take university courses or attend an appropriate seminar. At a more fundamental level, our friends can be our greatest teachers and tutors. I know that I have needed partners in my life who would stimulate me to think more clearly and less judgmentally, and my covenant partners have done that for me. Moreover, all of us need people who will prompt us to read more, reflect more deeply, and dream more boldly. Friends who are helping me to develop my mind in these ways are a profound gift!

As iron sharpens iron, a friend sharpens a friend.

—Proverbs 27:17

Chapter 17

Helping My Spirit

The most important thing in my life is my relationship with God. This is not only reflected in my friendships with Carson and Bob, it is the basis upon which we have established our relationship. We each want to make God our first priority, and we expect our faith to impact every area of our lives, including our friendships. We sometimes fail in this effort, and our lives don't always reflect this desire. But we know that at the core of each of our hearts there is, as stated in the Old Testament, an intention to love God "with our whole heart, soul, mind and strength" (Dueteronomy 6:6).

As I described in chapter 3, our desire for greater spiritual growth is what first gave us the impetus to create a covenant friendship. Since then, my friends have significantly impacted my own spiritual development. Carson and Bob have modeled for me how to live lives of consistency and commitment as men of God. They have aided me in developing practical spiritual disciplines, such as spending time with God on a regular basis and in the use of a prayer journal. Most importantly, their lives have reminded me that spirituality is a matter of the heart, not acts of religion.

It is our desire to know God better and to be faithful to him daily that prompts us, more than anything else, to continue our covenant together in friendship. I hope this chapter provides you with a glimpse of the important effect that our faith has had on our friendship and, conversely, the impact our friendship has had on our spiritual development.

Consistency and Conviction

I can think of certain people in my world whose company invigorates me, and when they leave, I am full of resolve, ideas, and intentions about God, self-improvement, and service to others.

I can also think of people in my world whose presence exhausts me. And when they leave, I am ready for a long, long, nap. . . . Our spiritual passion is strongly influenced by the people who populate our personal lives.[1]

A central aim of our covenant friendship is to invigorate and encourage one another in our journey of faith. In fact, the primary reason I first became interested in a covenant relationship was that I knew I needed encouragement in my spiritual life. To encourage is by definition to give courage, and that is one virtue I felt I lacked and hoped that I might gain as I walked together in faith with other men.

Why did I need a dose of spiritual courage? In part, because what I believe to be true and how I think we should live seem to be questioned by a majority in Western society. During my lifetime, the gap has substantially widened between what I understand to be God's standards for living and what our current culture views as the norm. When my grandfather was president of Dominion Construction, for example, he built a number of large buildings for clients on the basis of a handshake; there were no written contracts. Fifty years later, when I graduated from the Sauder School of Business at the University of British Columbia, most of my fellow students did not believe that it was possible to be both successful and honest in business. By that time, our family company had long since had to abandon doing business without a written contract.

Times have truly changed. North American culture, which was founded largely on Christian principles, has become predominently secular. As a result of this, honesty and integrity have been pushed to the side in favor of moral relativism. In an age of tolerance, the dominant thinking is that none of us can, or should, judge another, and that what was once regarded as a wrongful action can be the right action in a particular set of circumstances. It seems Christian principles have fallen to the wayside along with Western society's acknowledgment of the Christian faith.[2]

With this ethos, it has become increasingly unfashionable to follow Jesus. In fact, it is not even considered to be politically correct to mention his name publicly—except as part of a curse.

Christmas greetings have been replaced by "season's greetings" so as not to cause offense to those who are not Christian. In public schools, traditional Christmas concerts have now been given the more generic label of "winter holiday concerts."

Nonetheless, I believe that there is a personal God who created the universe and who loves us. This is either the truth or it isn't. No matter how much faith I have or what I believe, the truth about God is distinct from my opinion. If I believe I can fly but then jump off a building, it's quite likely that gravity will prove me wrong—regardless of how much faith I have in my ability to fly.

I am discouraged when people around me scoff at the notion of absolute truth. I know many intelligent individuals who have given up on the idea of truth, choosing instead to accept the notion that there is no such thing. I find this a rather curious position, since, by asserting that there is no absolute truth, one must actually proclaim to know an absolute truth. This is obviously a philosophical discussion that is beyond the scope of this book. However, the way society views truth has an enormous impact on determining what is moral and ethical, both in relationships and in commerce. Consequently, I find myself increasingly isolated from others in my views of business ethics, family norms, and standards of morality.

My relationship with Carson and Bob has helped me to be more confident in living out what I believe, regardless of the contrary views of others. This assistance has primarily come about as they have demonstrated courage and consistency in their own lives.

Bob Takes on Precedent-Setting Cases

Bob graduated from Trinity Western University (TWU) and several years ago was asked to lead a legal team to fight for this Christian-based university's right to grant education degrees. The British Columbia College of Teachers (BCCT), which governs the teachers in our province, wanted to withhold this right because of concerns that education graduates would be prejudiced against homosexuals as a result of the school's Christian focus. The BCCT reasoned that the university's "community standards," which all its students are required to adhere to, did not support homosexual behavior and would, therefore, produce "homophobic" teachers. This accusation was made in the absence of any evidence that TWU students were homophobic and in spite of the fact that they had developed a reputation as top-notch teachers. The case set a precedent on the law books of this province, one for which the defense of religious freedom was ultimately—and successfully—argued before the Supreme Court of Canada.

Bob found it extremely challenging as he prepared for this case, discussed it in the media, and argued his case—all against the tide of secular opinion. Because he believes that God made men and women for sexual union with each other in marriage and that the traditional family with a lifelong union between a man and a woman provides the best environment to raise children, Bob was routinely made to feel like a relic adrift on the sea of contemporary opinion. Nonetheless, the foundation of his faith and the prayers of many friends encouraged him to persevere. In the end, the Supreme Court of Canada ruled that TWU had the right confer education degrees. Bob had weathered the storm, having defended his Christian convictions to the highest court in the country. He wrote the following paragraphs about the benefits of having covenant friends in a world where expectations for performance are high and opposition hostile:

Bob: As someone who is in a position of leadership, it is often expected that I will have my act together spiritually. Prior to our covenant relationship, I didn't feel that I had anyone whom I could turn to, to admit that I felt inadequate. Having two men whom I can trust in this way has enabled me to be vulnerable about spiritual matters. It has given me the opportunity to process doubts, concerns, my deepest longings, and even my own personal faults and inadequacies without fear that they will hold me with any less esteem or value. As a matter of fact, I don't think there is any other place, outside of my marriage, where I have been given both the permission and the freedom to be who I am spiritually, without risking judgment or disappointment.

For me, this aspect of our covenant relationship best replicates or mirrors the relationship that we have with Jesus. He knows everything about me and still accepts me, just as my covenant partners do. When life is stressful, it is comforting to have a place to go where I can lay everything on the table without fear of recrimination or judgment.

Carson Takes on a Faith Challenge

Carson also faces challenges in living out his faith. As president of Arrow Leadership Ministries, he has a mandate to train and equip emerging Christian leaders to have a more effective impact in our world. For several years, and particularly in the aftermath of the 9/11 terrorist attacks, the financial underpinnings of this ministry were seriously shaken. It became necessary to cut staff, as well as Carson's own salary. During this time, Carson received numerous job offers that offered a higher salary and a more secure work environment. He made the decision to stay and carry on because he believed that he had been called to the work of Arrow, despite the difficulties.

In the midst of challenging circumstances, these friends have modeled for me something of what it means to walk the walk of a Christian in the twenty-first century. For my own part, I've been sensing God calling me to work toward an abortion-free Canada. This will undoubtedly require me to live out the courage of my convictions—it even took a certain amount of courage to put these last two sentences in print. However, I know that Bob and Carson will stand with me as I seek to live a public and private life that are both consistent with what I believe.

Weariness

Moses was one of the great spiritual leaders in Jewish history. Exodus 17 records how God miraculously granted the Israelite army success in a battle with their enemy as long as Moses kept his arms raised to God in prayer. As the struggle continued, the Bible records that "Moses's hands grew weary." The heaviness in his muscles gradually forced him to drop his arms to his side, therefore presenting a growing danger that the battle might be lost.

This was the cue for his closest friends and advisors, Aaron and Hur, to take action (Exodus 17:12). They found a stone for Moses to sit on, stood on either side of him and held up his arms, "so that his hands were steady until the going down of the sun." As a result of their practical assistance and support for Moses that day, the Israelites were victorious in their battle.

"What weariness would have made impossible if Moses had insisted on performing alone, the help of special friends made triumphant."[3] This is quite remarkable when one considers that Moses had previously been part of numerous extraordinary and supernatural events that brought him face to face with God's presence and power: God spoke to Moses from a burning bush, he used him to part the Red Sea and he gave him the Ten Commandments. Yet, despite these amazing experiences, Moses was like us—very human. He needed friends and, at times, he was unable to accomplish God's purpose without their assistance.

Like Moses, Bob has sometimes felt like he was fighting a battle in God's place or on God's behalf. For a time, Bob was also lead counsel on an infamous book-banning case in the public school system (a public school board refused to approve three books about same-sex families that some teachers wanted for resources in kindergarten classrooms). Eventually, this case also went to the Supreme Court of Canada and, like the TWU case, it was a high profile, ideologically charged case that was significant to the Canadian education system, as well as for religious and parental rights in Canada.

Overall, these cases were draining and all-consuming. When added to his already demanding legal practice and the responsibilities of family, he experienced more than an ordinary feeling of weariness. Bob often told us that he felt like giving up—not because he didn't believe in the causes but because the cumulative stress was gradually wearing him down. At this point, he says that just a phone call or a chance to pray or talk with one of us was "life-sustaining."

As Moses needed Aaron and Hur, Bob needed friends to stand with him. It was an honor for Carson and me to metaphorically hold Bob's arms up while he was in battle. We loved him, encouraged him, prayed for him, and Carson even made a special trip to Ottawa to support Bob as he successfully argued the TWU case before the Supreme Court of Canada.

In a similar way, Bob and I have supported Carson as he has faced the significant challenges of Arrow's financial situation and then grieved the death of his father during one year and his mother the next. These cumulative pressures caused Carson to become very weary, both emotionally and physically. Yet Bob and I have both been uniquely positioned to support Carson through these circumstances. Bob lightened Carson's load by helping with the legal issues related to executing Carson's mother's estate and the sale of the family home. I set aside three days to drive with Carson to his parents' former home to pack up boxes, clean out the garage, take garbage to the dump, and drive the U-Haul truck back home. As chairman of Carson's board, I arranged a retreat so the board members could gather around Carson to affirm, encourage, and support him. Carson has said that Aaron and Hur themselves couldn't have given him any better support!

Developing Spiritual Disciplines

Time with God

Over the years I have come to see that Bob and Carson's public faith is grounded in their regular times of private prayer and retreat. I know that the development of a spiritual life fundamentally requires finding times and places to connect with God but, like most people, I have found it difficult to accomplish this with the regularity and consistency that my heart desires.

More than twenty years ago, I made a commitment to make time for God each day, even if it was just five minutes. Yet, even with this minimalist approach, I was still unsuccessful in maintaining a daily time with God. This inconsistency continued until Carson encouraged me to try a different approach. He gave me a daily devotional book that radically rejuvenated my devotional life and enabled me to develop faithfulness in this aspect of my spiritual pilgrimage. The book, *A Guide to Prayers for All God's People* accomplished what nothing else had been able to do.[4] It gave me a flexible way to approach time alone with God each day. If I had just two or three minutes to spare, there was a daily routine that I could readily apply. On the other hand, if I had twenty to thirty minutes to read and pray, there was ample material to guide me into greater depth with God. Using this tool has helped me to regularly reflect, pray, and read my Bible. In short, it has refreshed my spirit and enabled me to learn and grow spiritually.

At times my progress seems slow, but as I learn more about Jesus, I am beginning to think and act more as he would like me to. A breakthrough in achieving my goal to meet with God on a regular basis has been accomplished, at least in part, by the example of my two friends and Carson's practical, habit-changing gift.

Retreats

As mentioned in the previous chapter, the three of us have begun going on annual retreats to Westminster Abbey, a beautiful monastery overlooking the Fraser River east of Vancouver. This has enabled me to experience the sense of renewal and perspective that comes from withdrawing and slowing down for a day or two. A tool that has been particularly helpful in stimulating these times of contemplation is a journal that Bob gave to me. I wasn't accustomed to recording my innermost thoughts and feelings, so at first I wrote in fits and starts. Most of my early entries were a confusing jumble of raw emotions. Complaints against God were common, as were rants against others for their treatment of me. It seems that I took to heart the words of C. S. Lewis, "Whenever you are fed up with life, start writing; ink is the great cure for all human ills, as I have found out long ago."[5]

Journaling

As time has passed, I have grown more comfortable with the process of journaling, and my entries have become more balanced. I have discovered that a personal journal can be a great private discipline, and I now use it to record my deepest reflections on a regular basis. I find that the simple act of writing down my thoughts and prayers helps to slow me down and focus my thoughts and emotions. As I write and contemplate my emotions, I am able to gain much-needed perspective and understanding. For example, I recently felt stuck and somewhat frustrated as I struggled with my tendency to criticize. At the time, things had not been going well for Alison and me in our marriage. The less happy I was with myself, the more I tended to criticize Alison. When I realized this, I became even more discouraged and, as I battled these feelings, I wrote the following:

> *Journal:* I feel like I am in chains. Help me to be like the
>   Apostle Paul, rejoicing in my imprisonment.
> *Prayer:* Do a supernatural work in me—put out the fire of
>   anger. I am in prison—help me sing from behind bars!
> *Journal:* Until I am perfect . . . let me never criticize another!

It was only as I wrote those words down that I recognized a key to unlocking my relationship with Alison. I needed to abandon my critical spirit. I had tried to not criticize, because I knew how destructive criticism could be in a marriage. But as I reflected on what I wrote, I realized that my attitude needed to change before I could change my behavior—and to accomplish a change in my attitude, I needed God's help.

Unfortunately, not all my journaling efforts have paid off with such dramatic insights. But journaling now feels more like recording a conversation that I might have had with my dad. My pages are filled with phrases such as, "Help me to be more patient," "Guide me as I work with Alison to prepare our family budget," and "Help me to fall in love with our children." As I have worked through my emotions and feelings through journaling, my relationships with members of my family have improved. The kids may never realize it, but the depth and growth of our relationship is largely rooted in my efforts to take time to withdraw, to reflect, to journal, and to pray.

What is the lesson in all this? Carson and Bob have helped me to have a faith that is more real because they live out their faith in a way that I want to emulate. Along the way, they have introduced me to practical disciplines like retreat and journaling, both of which have proved to be invaluable to my spiritual growth.

Spirituality Is about the Internal

In our covenant relationship, the focus of our spiritual pursuits is spirituality, not religion. That is to say, the focus is on internal growth, not outward ritual alone. Much religious activity seems to focus on the temporal or the material. In the Old Testament, for example, religious activities included strict keeping of the law, sacrifices at the temple, covering one's head, and giving alms and sacrifices. Regardless of what religious tradition one considers, the focus tends to be on outward behavior. Some traditions have since changed, but there remains a tendency for all of us to reduce our spiritual lives to a list of do's and don'ts. Sadly this limits our religious experience to a set of activities to perform, prayers to pray, or services and programs to attend. No wonder we find religion to be lifeless and unable to feed our spiritual hunger.

Certainly, some activities are worthwhile and may even lead to spiritual growth. However, the truth is that these activities don't represent the essence of spirituality. God is much more interested in relationships than in performance. He desires righteous hearts more than righteous acts (although both are important) and he is looking for acts of true devotion, not just the appearance of it. As a result, we need to be on guard against the tendency to live moral lives that are not in any real sense of the word *spiritual.* Lest this sound arrogant, I don't mean to suggest that we've got it all together. Rather, by encouraging each other to know God and not merely perform religious acts, we can remind one another to turn our eyes heavenward.

Conclusion

Our society worships tolerance, yet tolerance toward those who name the name of Jesus is often found lacking. In this environment, it requires courage to live out one's faith, and the resulting battle can make us weary. Therefore, friends who will encourage and support us in our faith are increasingly important.

Many assume that spirituality and friendship have no connection at all and that spirituality is strictly a personal matter. Yet, my own spiritual development has been profoundly impacted by my friends. By bringing our spiritual issues, both good and bad, out into the light, we openly talk and pray together about our struggles and gain strength and courage as we walk together, no longer alone in the journey.

Train yourself to be godly. For physical training is of some value, but godliness has value for all things, holding promise for the present life and the life to come.

—Timothy 4:7b–8

Part IV

How Friendship Helps Our Spirit

Friendship has been described as "the happiest and most human of all loves; the crown of life."[1] But much of that luster has been lost in our fast-paced society, and this is particularly true for men. Work schedules, family commitments, community involvements, sporting activities, and the "urgent" messages that continuously bombard us via e-mail, pagers, and cell phones all seem to tell us that we don't have time—for friendship.

We inevitably face a choice: Do we give in to the "tyranny of the urgent," or do we invest in relationships? Friendship takes time and work. We will never experience the transforming power of friendship if we don't choose to take time for friendship. In making decisions about how to spend our time, it has been helpful and inspiring to study the life of Jesus.

Chapter 18 examines how Jesus prioritized and managed his limited amount of time to maximize his influence on others. It then suggests that we use him as a model for our earthly friendships.

In chapter 19, I provide several practical suggestions for initiating and building relationships that will last for a lifetime.

Chapter 18

Jesus As a Model for Friendship and Life

The Messiah, Handel's classic Christmas oratorio, has familiarized many of us with some of the names commonly used to describe Jesus and his character: "Wonderful, Counselor, Almighty God, Everlasting Father, Prince of Peace, King of Kings, Lord of Lords, Emmanuel, God with Us."[1] The Bible also describes Jesus as the creator and sustainer of the universe, the savior of the world, a great teacher, and a healer.

Growing up in a church-going family, I was familiar with these names and descriptions of Jesus. As a result, I had no problem thinking of Jesus as God's son and as a miracle worker—even as a role model for leadership. But it wasn't until I was in my early twenties that I was presented with the idea that Jesus could also be a model for friendship. This was a revolutionary idea for me. I was intrigued by the idea that Jesus had fostered the same kinds of friendships that I wanted to develop in my life.

I was introduced to this concept when I attended a weekend retreat with fellow college undergrads at Keats Island, just off the coast of British Columbia. Chuck Ferguson, a former Young Life leader, was the speaker. In a series of talks he identified four spheres of relationships that Jesus had. He then encouraged us to use them as a model for our own friendships. I share them with you now with the hope that you will do the same.

1. *Jesus spent time with God.* Jesus regularly withdrew from others to study the Scriptures and to pray. He took time to be in God's presence early in the morning, when the world around him was still and quiet. This time was the ultimate source of his strength for each day, and this dependence on time alone with God became even more evident as the time of his own crucifixion and death drew near. In his darkest hours, he went to the Garden of Gethsemane to pray.

Obviously, if we want to grow in our spiritual lives we need to take time to study God's word, pray, and learn to be quiet in God's presence. Gary Thomas writes, "The spiritual life is impossible in a heart full of noise and occupation. God will not fill a heart that has no room."[2] Being still is difficult and, as I discussed in a previous chapter, to get away and be quiet requires discipline and determination. If we accomplish this, we will be rewarded with the perspective and strength that we need to face the day ahead.

2. *Jesus spent time in worship.* One of the most common images of Jesus in the Gospels is that of him surrounded by crowds of people. Without a Dodger Stadium or Wrigley Field to hold his crowds, or even modern advertising to draw them in, he nonetheless managed to gather multitudes of people around him. They came to satisfy their hunger with his life-sustaining words.

If we are interested in developing the spiritual side of our lives, we need to be part of a community where God is honored and worshiped. The psalmist says, "I was glad when they said unto me, 'Let us go into the house of the Lord together'" (Psalm 122:1). Even though Jesus had serious concerns about the hypocrisy and duplicity of many who attended synagogue, he still went to the house of God to worship, choosing to overlook others' imperfections in order to focus his gaze toward his Father in heaven.

3. *Jesus spent time with a small group.* Jesus had a profound impact on thousands of people through his preaching and teaching. Yet, despite the overwhelming attention and needs of the crowds, he still made time with his twelve disciples his top priority. For three years, he invested his life in this small group of men, teaching them by word and by example. He showed them how to live a godly life and how to teach others to follow the same path.

Over the last few decades, small-group Bible studies and prayer groups have become increasingly popular and instrumental in church growth. As an example, I am told that Kampala Pentecostal Church in Uganda has divided up its eleven thousand members into cell groups consisting of ten persons each. I believe it is this small-group phenomenon that lies at the heart of this church's strength.

The mutual support and nurture that can come from a small group of people honestly sharing around God's word can be life-changing. As we wrestle with life's challenges and address its opportunities, it can be extremely helpful to have a cadre of close associates who can be a reference point and source of strength for us. Following Jesus as an example, I have gained strength over the years by attending small group Bible studies.

4. *Jesus spent time with a few close friends.* Within his group of disciples, Jesus shared a particularly close relationship with three men—Peter, James, and John. Matthew's Gospel tells us that these were among the first disciples that Jesus called to follow him. His journey then became *their* journey and, as David Benner writes, "this is what true friends do. They accompany each other on life's journey."[3]

Jesus invited the disciples to join him during most significant events of his life and, after Jesus had been crucified and buried in a garden tomb, Peter and John were among the first to race into the tomb, only to discover that Jesus was no longer there. He had indeed risen from the dead.

There is not much said about the nature of Jesus' friendship with Peter, James, and John. However, given their presence at certain notable occasions and the conversations which were recorded, I infer that these men were like his inner cabinet, his most trusted advisors. More importantly, it appears that they were his constant companions, even during his darkest hours.

As we peer through these four spheres of friendship, we see that Jesus is indeed a great model for how we can develop relationships that will sustain and transform us. If we should pattern our lives after his example, we should take time alone with God, take time to worship, and find time to be involved in a small group. Most importantly, as Jesus demonstrated in his own life, we would also be wise to invest time in developing close, transparent relationships with two or three others who will be there for us like Peter, James, and John were for him.

Developing Character

Jesus is also worth emulating with respect to the type of men we should become and the kind of character we should seek to develop. Over the years, Carson, Bob, and I have tried to emulate and develop the following characteristics that were exemplified by Jesus:

1. *Compassion.* Jesus had great love and compassion for everyone he met. For example, in Luke 7:13 we read that Jesus met a woman whose son had recently died. His heart was "filled with compassion" toward her and, as a result he reached out and touched the boy's body, bringing him back to life.

2. *Unselfish love.* Jesus met a Samaritan woman one day when he went to the well to draw water. In those days, it was politically incorrect for a man to even talk to a woman in those circumstances. Moreover, the Jews and Samaritans were bitter enemies, and it would have been folly for a Jew to even speak to a Samaritan. Yet Jesus rose above these constraints to reach out to her, to engage in conversation with her, and to offer this thirsty woman a drink from the "well of life." He did not judge her based on her gender or her culture. Instead, he saw her accurately as a child of God made in his image. Wouldn't relationships in our world be transformed if more men would look past people's outward appearances and backgrounds to reach out in love through simple conversation?

3. *Tenderness.* Jesus' disciples often grew impatient with him when there were huge crowds around him. They even tried to keep the little children away from him. Jesus rebuked this action by saying, "Let the little children come to me, and do not hinder them.... Anyone who will not receive the kingdom of God like a little child will never enter it" (Mark 10:14–15).

Most of us are too busy playing Superman at the office to take the time to get to know our own children. Many of us are inclined to have such an inflated sense of self-importance and are so focused on our career goals that we easily overlook our responsibilities to our children. I have been praying for several years that God will enable me to fall deeply in love with our children. Happily, I believe my heart is growing increasingly tender toward them. As my love grows, I know our relationship will be transformed. I am glad that God is helping me to develop a more tender heart for our children.

4. *Forthrightness.* When Jesus entered the temple in Jerusalem and found it filled with moneychangers and sellers who were cheating the people, he forcefully threw them out of the temple, saying, "You have made my Father's house a den of thieves" (Mark 11:17).

Jesus wasn't just in a bad mood that day, nor did he succumb to anger and fly off the handle. He behaved as he did when he identified the transgressions of injustice and theft, and saw the desecration of God's house of worship. He then called the guilty parties to account. Our places of work and worship would be similarly transformed if men held each other to account and stood up for what was right.

5. *Service.* In Jesus' day, washing the feet of visitors who had traveled in their sandals through the dusty dirty streets was a filthy job and typically delegated to a slave. Yet during the last meal Jesus spent with his disciples before his death, he washed their feet in an amazing and symbolic act of service. Most men I know are more interested in being served than in serving others, whether at work or at home. Yet wouldn't our relationships be enhanced greatly if we could learn to regularly put on "the towel of service"?

6. *Forgiveness.* Peter denied knowing Jesus on three separate occasions in the hours leading up to the crucifixion. Yet Jesus still referred to Peter as the "rock" and announced that it was "upon this rock" that he would establish his church (Matthew 16:18). That is, instead of recriminations and criticism for Peter's lack of faith and unfaithfulness, Jesus affirmed and restored Peter to a position of leadership. We all make mistakes and sometimes, even when we apologize for the wrongs we have done, we can still suffer under the disapproving eye of an unforgiving friend. Our emotional baggage would be lightened considerably if we abandoned grudges and learned to genuinely and openly forgive.

One could go on at great length to describe the characteristics of Jesus that are worthy of emulating. Indeed, Jesus' revolutionary character challenges us to be radically different in our modern world, where desires for success and position dominate so much of our current thinking.

Conclusion

This book is for everyone who is interested in discovering the pleasure of friendships that go beyond the superficial. I also hope it is clear that the source of strength for my covenant friends and me is our relationship with God through Jesus Christ. We all try to live a life that reflects that of Jesus, and this includes his relationships. This is why we are all committed to build into our lives time for solitude, time for worship, time for study, and time for close friends.

I encourage you to invest in all these areas. Most importantly, I urge you to invest in a friendship with God. For it is the creator and author of life who, ultimately, holds the key to all meaningful relationships in this life and in the life beyond.

Let us love one another, for love comes from God.

—1 John 4:7

Chapter 19

Making Friendship Happen!

By now, I hope you are convinced that intentional friendship is worth a try. But how do you get started? There are no magic formulas, shortcuts, or guarantees in the realm of relationships. But there are some practical principles that can assist you to deepen your experience of friendship.

Make a List

As described in chapter 2, Alison and I were planning our wedding, when we sat down with a piece of paper and listed names of candidates to be my best man. That was when I realized that I really didn't know anyone well enough to expect them to play such a role. That was the first impetus for being intentional about developing friendships. Alison and I then decided that I would choose two men who shared my faith and values to develop an intentional friendship. I could never have predicted how significantly my life would be affected and enriched by this one decision. You could begin a similar journey by grabbing a pen and paper and making a list of men you know who might be candidates for a deeper friendship.

Get on Your Knees

Why not ask God for help in this process? I did. After Alison and I determined which two men I would approach to pursue friendships, I prayed and asked that God would go before me and open their hearts to the idea. It made a difference. When I approached them, I didn't feel alone or that I was out to lunch by making such a request of my friends. Rather, I had an unseen, all-powerful helper on this new path that I had chosen. In the years since then, my friendships have derived their strength and longevity, in part, from being rooted in a mutual desire to grow in our understanding of God and in our desire to serve God.

Take Initiative

As you were growing up, your parents likely told you that to have a friend, you had to be a friend. This hasn't changed over the years. It remains true for both children and adults, but it is risky. When you step out and offer yourself in friendship, there are no guarantees that the favor will be returned. Most ventures of any value are accompanied by risk. Remind yourself that there is also a risk in not working toward better friendships. If you don't establish friendships or work toward more positive ones, the risk of loneliness and aloneness also run pretty high. Call one or two guys on your list. Take the initiative and get together with them for a run, a coffee, or a lunch, and tell them about your idea.

Twenty years ago, I was astonished at the responses I received from the two men I approached. Dean Taylor and Mike Simms didn't think that working toward a deeper friendship was an odd request. Instead, they indicated that they wanted the same, and together we began to pursue closer relationships.

Get Together Often

If you want to build a friendship, there is no substitute for spending time together. As a young father, I recall being advised that if I wanted to build a friendship with my children that would survive the tumultuous teen years, I should have breakfast with them at least once a week before school and I should meet each of them regularly for dates. These occasions gave us a chance to get to know each other better, and now that most of our children have graduated from high school and moved away from home, I can see how vitally important this was. We wouldn't have shared as much time together if we hadn't been intentional in getting together for quality time.

Similarly, friendships are cultivated by spending time together and, in most cases, it is ideal to get together once a week. There is no set formula, but being together regularly is essential. Without such contact, your friendship will wither, just like an unattended houseplant.

Agree on Guidelines for Friendships

Think about it. All formal groups (corporations, associations, nations, churches, and communities) have guidelines to assist them in building relationships. It can be a constitution, a bill of rights, laws of governance, or even a set of bylaws for a charitable organization. Each of these sets of rules acknowledges that building long-term relationships requires guiding principles to shape their direction.

Without guidelines, relationships have no context or direction. Think about how futile a football team would be without assigned positions, or how ineffectual a corporation would be without clearly defined roles for its employees. Similarly, without a basic set of ground rules or common agreement of purpose, relational growth is subject to chance or happenstance. Friendships, then, become directionless and potentially meaningless. Establishing guidelines may be as simple as agreeing to meet regularly for mutual encouragement. In his book, *Locking Arms,* author Stu Weber suggests a simple structure for creating friendships, called *The Four A's:*

1. *Acceptance:* Accept the other person exactly as he is.
2. *Affirmation:* Encourage one another by accentuating each other's positive attributes.
3. *Accountability:* Earn the right to ask the hard questions. Accountability isn't immediate—it grows over time.
4. *Authority:* Submit mutually to the standards and values of God's word.[1]

As explained in chapter 3, Carson, Bob, and I have created our own eight-point covenant. The following summarizes each aspect of our covenant of friendship:

Covenant of AFFIRMATION

There is nothing you have done or will do that will make me stop loving you. I may not agree with your actions, but

I will love you as a person and do all I can to hold you up in God's affirming love.

Covenant of AVAILABILITY

I will make time, energy, insight, and possessions freely available when needed and in proper relationship to my other covenant commitments. As part of this availability, I pledge my time on a regular basis, whether in prayer or in an agreed upon meeting time.

Covenant of PRAYER

I covenant to regularly pray for you, believing that our caring Father wishes his children to pray for one another and ask him for the blessings they need and the desires of their hearts.

Covenant of OPENNESS

I promise to strive to become a more open, vulnerable person, disclosing my hurts to you. I desire to trust you with my problems and my dreams. This is to affirm your worth to me as a person.

Covenant of HONESTY

I will try to mirror back to you what I am hearing you say, and my feelings and thoughts in response. If this means risking pain for either of us, I will trust our mutual covenant enough to take that risk, realizing it is in "speaking the truth in love that we grow up in every way into Christ who is the head" (Ephesians 4:15). I will try to express this honestly in a sensitive and controlled manner and to monitor it according to what I perceive your needs to be.

Covenant of SENSITIVITY

Even as I desire to be known and understood by you, I covenant to be sensitive to you and to your needs to the best of my ability. I will try to hear you, see you, and feel where you are and to draw you out of discouragement or withdrawal.

Covenant of CONFIDENTIALITY

I promise to keep confidential whatever is shared within the confines of our mutual covenant in order to protect the atmosphere of openness and trust.

Covenant of ACCOUNTABILITY

I covenant to use the gifts that God has given me for your benefit. If I discover areas of my life that are negatively affected by my own misdoings or by the scars inflicted by others, I will seek Christ's liberating power through the Holy Spirit and through you so that I might better serve God and fulfill my covenants to you. I am accountable to you in my commitment to become what God has designed me to be in his loving creation.

Our covenant is uniquely tailored to the needs and desires of the three of us, so the specifics may not be appropriate for you and your friends. However, you may want to use our covenant— or *The Four A's*—as a starting point for creating your own set of guidelines for intentional friendship.

A Word of Caution

Covenant friendship isn't about grabbing the nearest potential friend and immediately diving into a covenant. Carson and I had known each other for more than fifteen years, and Bob and I for more than ten years before we decided to create a covenant friendship. In other words, we had already built solid relationships before we decided to crystallize them in a covenant relationship. Moreover, we had already been meeting together without any written guidelines for quite some time before we decided to formalize things. Just like a healthy dating relationship may lead to marriage, a period of "getting to know you," and a deepening of commitment should preface a formalized relationship. As you consider this, keep the following points in mind:

1. *Friendship takes time.* You will have to carve out time from your schedule to be with people. There are no shortcuts. If you want to have close friendships, you have to invest time. Be patient.
2. *Friendship takes work.* Like strong marriages, friendships don't just happen. They require a commitment over the long haul—in good times and bad.

Conclusion

The kind of friendship that I am advocating is radical. It goes against the grain of today's society, and it involves a deliberate choice to invest time in friendship. For most men, this means a shift in thinking and priorities. It will mean taking time away from some other things that currently occupy your time. It may also mean learning to listen and talk about deeper things. Each man that chooses to undertake this paradigm shift will have the opportunity to find meaningful friendship. In turn, these friendships have the potential to change us—in body, mind and spirit—and to inspire us to be better husbands, better fathers, and better leaders. If you could bottle such a power and sell it, it would be worth its weight in gold—kind of like friends.

Jesus says . . .

Greater love has no one than this; that one lay down his life for his friends.

This is my command: Love each other.

—John 15:13, 17

Appendix:

Commonly Asked Questions about Our Friendship

This appendix deals with some of the most frequently asked questions that both men and their wives have regarding our covenant friendship.

1. What does your wife think? Doesn't your commitment to each other compete with your marriage—and perhaps even undermine your marriage?

Here is a response from each of our wives:

My wife, Alison: "I'm not at all threatened by it—in fact, I'm comforted. David's commitment to being accountable to friends indicates that he cares enough about his life to grow, and any personal growth for him will help us in our marriage."

Bob's wife, Renae: "I know Bob gets great support from his friends and that enables him to be able to love me and our children in a better way."

Carson's wife, Brenda: "I cannot be all things to my husband. I want him to have other people to turn to for accountability and perspective. This doesn't prevent him from being accountable to me, nor does it prevent him from getting my perspective. I appreciate knowing that I am not alone in helping him to be all he can be. I don't know if I've stated it strongly enough, but I really value what happens between the three of you. When Carson comes home from being with you, I can see that he is energized by it and more fulfilled. I just love to see that in him!"

One of the main reasons that Carson, Bob, and I entered into our covenant was that we wanted to help each other grow in our marriages and to become better husbands. In the language of our covenant, our commitment of availability to each other is to be "in proper relationship to our other covenant commitments." This specifically addresses our prior commitment to our spouses and affirms that our commitment to our marriages remains preeminent.

Coming at it from another angle, counselors are quick to say that a marriage partner cannot meet all one's needs. If you find a man who says his wife is his only friend, then you'll likely find a wife who wants her husband to find a friend. Wives cannot meet all the emotional needs of their husbands, just as husbands cannot meet all the emotional needs of their wives.

How we manage our covenant relationships in light of our marriages is such a critical issue. I asked Roy Cook's wife, Evelyn, to comment on Roy's fifty-year covenant friendship with Doug Coe, chair of the annual Presidential Prayer Breakfast in Washington, D.C.

> *Evelyn Cook:* My husband's close friendships strengthen our marriage, not weaken it. I recognize that all the men are on my side, wanting Roy to treat me well, love me well, and remain faithful to me. However, some spouses do feel threatened if they can't relate to the vision the guys have or to their need to be together. Sometimes women are worried about confidentiality, and some of the confidences being shared. To counterbalance such fears, men should resolve to make their wives feel connected to what is going on and reassure them of the integrity of men involved and the goals of the relationship. Don't share private information about your life, unless your wife gives you permission and be sure to share your heart and what you are doing with your wife. Demonstrate that she is first in your life, before other men!

These comments highlight how important it is that we explain to our spouses what we are doing in our covenant and why we should constantly ask for their input. This will ensure that our marriage commitment remains a higher priority than our friendships, as it should.

2. How does your friendship affect time with your family?

We believe that friendship should complement our family life rather than compete with our families for our attention. Friendships can make a man a better father and husband as long as the principal focus of his life remains his family.

In chapter 13, I emphasized that one of our goals is to become better parents through the help of our covenant partners. If friendships at their core are dedicated to helping with family life, then positive results can be achieved. But let us not be naïve. Friendships take time, and there is a real danger that the company of good friends can detract from family time. Think about the hours that men consume playing golf on a Saturday morning. Those five hours with friends is a huge investment. In comparison, the amount of time that the average father spends listening or talking meaningfully with his children would pale in comparison. Friendships that constructively challenge us to spend more time with our families have the potential to produce better fathers and better families.

3. What about male friendship and homosexuality?

As our modern society increasingly tolerates homosexual behavior, I feel that I need to emphasize that the type of friendships espoused in this book are not in any way sexual in nature. I believe that we are created by God, and that heterosexual, monogamous relationships are the intended context for our sexual fulfillment and the rearing of families.

Yet our culture's current assumptions continue to fuel questions and fears about sexuality being present in male friendship. Dr. Mitch Whitman, a psychologist and counselor who specializes in sexual issues, offers the following helpful observations:

> Many men are fearful of being identified as "gay" if they develop an intimate or affectionate relationship with another man. Further, with some there may be a fear that such affection might lead to some sort of genital activity. This latter issue is, I think, demeaning to men if generalized. It also suggests for

a particular individual, the message that self-control, self-efficacy, and sexual integration are not possible. This is a lie about men in general or specific men in particular.[1]

There is no need to flee from healthy male friendships simply because a portion of our society stridently tolerates homosexual behavior. I think that as Christians we can assert a higher ground, both theologically and experientially. I currently have several friendships with men toward whom I feel great affection, love, and commitment, just as I have had in the past. It would be a tragedy if I or other men eschewed quality friendships simply because of this nebulous fear of the relationship becoming sexual.

The fear of becoming a homosexual by developing close friendships with other men poses a real challenge to modern male friendships. Intimate (emotional, social, intellectual, non-sexual) relationships with fellow men can greatly enrich each other's lives, enhance the experience of true community, and foster better mental and emotional health.

4. What if I'm too busy for friends?

We are all limited by the constraints of time. Many of us can easily argue that we are too busy with our work, families, or community involvement to have time for significant friendships. Consequently, we may need to give up some things to invest in quality relationships.

There is a story about a professor who held a Mason jar before his class and challenged them to put ten big rocks inside the glass receptacle. He then asked them whether the vessel was full. Most of them responded that it was. But then he poured gravel into it and asked the same question. Now they weren't sure how to respond. To further drive home his point, the professor then poured sand in and, subsequently, water.

When I first heard this, I thought that the moral was that you can always fit more into any given day. The wise professor has a different lesson for us. He wanted to make the point that we can only fit the big rocks into our lives if we put them in first. If you decide to invest in meaningful friendships, you also have to determine that these relationships will be some of the big rocks of your life. Making friendships a priority can be done—and it is worth it.

5. How does friendship relate to career and other priorities?

My dad died recently and, as I prepared his eulogy and looked back over his life, it was easy to see what mattered most to him. He had achieved financial success and become a prominent business leader. He had a beautiful home in Vancouver, a summer home on Keats Island, and a winter residence in Palm Springs. He had a fabulous boat, a fine car, prominent board directorships, and the respect of his community. But impressive as all this is, it was the quality and depth of his friendships that marked him as a person. One boyhood friend from grade 8 had remained a friend and confidant for seventy years; another close friendship spanned more than forty years.

Dave Phillips, a world-class athlete and executive with Focus on the Family (Canada), says, "Investing in friendship may even be a good idea financially. Although difficult to prove, it does stand to reason that, if you develop strong friendships, you will experience a greater cross-pollination of ideas and wisdom, which can provide greater balance in your life. If you are living life in balance you are more responsive to those around you and therefore apt to be more successful vocationally."

The more we learn about the value of contributing to the nourishment and encouragement of friends, the more productive we will be for ourselves, our families, and in our jobs. When we learn, with the help of friends, to think about and care for others we may become more valuable employers or employees.

6. How does one build friendships?

Our friendship covenant did not spring forth overnight but was something that grew over many years before we decided to formalize it. Such a progression makes sense. After all, it is likely that the covenant of marriage as we know it—the most intimate and important relationship that most of us have in our lives today—does not just happen overnight. It may begin with a casual encounter that later leads to a romantic dinner, which then leads to spending increasing amounts of time together and finally to a mutual commitment. In the best of cases, a solid foundation is built before a lifetime commitment is made.

In initiating an intentional, purposeful relationship, I advocate what I discussed in chapters 2 and 19. Make a list of guys that you think might be valuable friends on a deeper level, think about it, pray about it, and then take the initiative to get together and discuss friendship at a deep level. Intentional covenant friendship requires a willingness to take action.

7. Do you need mutual interests to establish a friendship?

I once thought that friendship was built on common interests. While there is no doubt that shared interests or hobbies can assist in its formation, I now believe shared values—and not shared activities—are the cornerstone of a friendship. Consider the most prominent friendship in the Bible, that of David and Jonathan. "One was a prince; the other was a shepherd. They didn't necessarily have the same skills or talents, but they had the same values."[2] Yet despite the differences in backgrounds and gifts, David and Jonathan were soulmates. Stu Weber describes this relationship: "The soul is that invisible part of us that combines our minds and wills and emotions. Here were two men whose minds believed the same truth, whose wills were under the same course, whose emotions burned at the same injustices." In other words, "they marched to the same tune. They were headed in the same direction. They even dreamed about the same things."[3]

In our own covenant, Bob, Carson, and I have to be creative in finding ways of sharing our lives together. We've begun taking holidays together with our families—everyone enjoys being out on the water, swimming in a pool, or having a summertime barbecue. Similarly we can all enjoy a movie together or, if I twist some arms a little, we can play charades. The point is that we don't have to be running marathons together or in the same book club. Shared values and/or a shared faith are the basic requirements.

8. What about a midlife crisis?

In today's world, many of us go through a midlife reassessment, a.k.a. "crisis," where we may feel as though we are coming apart at the seams. Some have described the experience as a period of second adolescence, where questions of identity once again emerge and men seriously question their accomplishments in life. In other words, we reevaluate our success as husbands and fathers and our contributions to church, community, and the world. We begin to sense a longing for significance and wonder if our lives will make a difference in this world.

As men go through this midlife reassessment, they are sometimes tempted to discard things that shouldn't be discarded, such as families, marriages, and other things of immeasurable value. Therefore, this is a key time for men to invest in meaningful relationships with other men so that they will have friends who will stand with them and support them as they weather the storms that self-doubt and an awareness of one's own mortality inevitability bring.

Although it's never too late to begin thinking about meaningful friendships, I would encourage every man to invest in friendship at an early age, because the deeper the roots go in a tree, the stronger it will be. Only solid, deeply-rooted friendships will last the test of time.

9. What about disappointments?

Are you setting yourself up for disappointment by investing in friendship? Won't friends inevitably let down you down? The answer to these questions is both yes and no.

Yes, we are all going to be let down by our friends. But the same could be said of sporting activities. We've all been let down by teammates, and we are all guilty of letting teammates down. However, looking back I wouldn't choose to have never played any rugby games simply because there was a chance one of my teammates would let me down. In fact, as I look back, more often than not, my teammates have not let me down but have supported me. As a result of playing with teams, some of the highlights of my life include championship wins.

It may sound trite, but nothing ventured does indeed result in nothing gained. Friends have disappointed me from time to time, just as I know I have disappointed friends. Yet I am determined that the inevitability of disappointment will not keep me from enjoying the benefits and blessings that come from friendship. Furthermore, when disappointments come, we can use them to build stronger bonds, learning to apologize, confess, and mutually forgive each other.

10. Are there risks of possessiveness, codependency, or dependency?

Codependent relationships, in simplest terms, are those where we take someone else's problems and make them our own. For example, if I were to cover up for a friend's drinking problem by making excuses for him. Obviously, this is a danger in any close relationship. But Carson, Bob, and I have committed to speaking the truth to one another, rather than hiding the truth from each other. This serves as an antidote to codependency. Furthermore, there is an advantage to being a group of three. If one of us were to begin to be codependent with another, the third member of our triumvirate would likely have the necessary perspective to root this out.

Dependent relationships develop when one person becomes dependent on the other over a period of time. Again, we are somewhat protected from this because we are a threesome. Moreover, our focus as friends is outward and upward, as we try to encourage one another in our vertical relationship with God, our relationships with our families, and our roles in the world. As such, we are continually trying to encourage one another to become the best we can be rather than allowing each other to lean heavily on one another.

Possessiveness in friendship is something we can all relate to from our earliest days on the elementary school playground. Friends can become jealous when another gains the attention or the time of a close friend. I must confess that since both Carson and Bob live in Langley, I sometimes feel that I'm on the outside looking in. However, the distance dynamic has helped me to grow as a person as I have had to face this niggling, petty, concern. One of the things that has helped me the most has been the knowledge that these men, in writing, have committed to me for life. I can look at our covenant, read it, trust it, and *know* that it is true. They have promised to be there for me, and I need only ask for their time, support, and friendship.

It has also helped me to remember that friendship is something that is freely given. Whenever I feel small or possessive, I try to challenge myself to think of what can I do for them. How can I love them? The answer is usually apparent. I am seldom doing enough for them, and so I need not worry about whether they are doing enough for me. This encourages me to invest in caring more for them.

11. Do you share financial information with each other?

Bob, Carson, and I haven't talked a lot about finances. This isn't surprising, since there are so many other issues in life to deal with. Yet we are open to discuss this subject and when one of us has had a pressing financial circumstance, we were able to talk about it and provide perspective and encouragement.

12. Do you need to be at the same economic level?

We are definitely not all at the same economic level. A pastor's income is very different from that of the chief executive of a construction company that has annual revenues approaching $300 million. I watched my father have friendships with people from all walks of life, and I think this is as it should be. I recall when Alison and I were invited for an evening cruise on billionaire Jimmy Pattison's boat. There were another fifteen couples present, one of which was a senior banker who had a six-figure income and golf memberships that put him in an elite class in our community. But another guest was the parkade attendant from Jimmy's office building. Each of us was invited to share, for five minutes, a life story that we thought would be of interest to the rest of the group. Our financial circumstances might have been different, and our incomes definitely were, but we all had life experiences that were rich and worth sharing.

Notes

Introduction

1. C. S. Lewis, *The Four Loves* (Harcourt Brace, 1960), 57.

Chapter 1

1. Peter Legge, *How to Soar with the Eagles* (Burnaby, B.C., Canada: Eaglet Publishing, 1992), 199.
2. Robert D. Putnam, *Bowling Alone* (New York: Simon & Schuster, 2000), 95.
3. Dave Phillips, personal communication.
4. George Sears, *Man's Search for Male Friendship,* unpublished D. Min. thesis (Fuller Seminary, 1997), 29.
5. Lewis, *The Four Loves,* 60.
6. More information about *Promise Keepers* is available at www. promisekeepers.org.
7. Located north of Chicago, Willowcreek is arguably one of the largest, most influential churches in North America today.
8. Bill Hybels, *Becoming a Contagious Christian* (Grand Rapids, Mich.: Zondervan, 1994), 96.
9. Vince Lombardi, in Stu Weber, *Tender Warrior: God's Intention for a Man* (Sisters, Ore.: Multnomah Publishing, 1999), 76.

Chapter 2

1. Lewis, *The Four Loves,* 121.
2. Peter Legge, personal communication.

Chapter 3

1. David Benner, *Sacred Companions: The Gift of Spiritual Friendship and Direction* (Downers Grove, Ill.: Inter-Varsity Press, 2002), 63.

Chapter 4

1. Larry Crabb, *Connecting* (Nashville: Word Publishing, 1997), 13.
2. John Gray, *Men Are from Mars, Women Are from Venus* (New York: HarperCollins, 1992), 56.

3. Nate Adams, "Honey, What Should I Wear?" *New Man Magazine,* March/April 1999.

4. John Wooden, *A Lifetime of Observations on and off the Court* (New York: Contemporary Books, 1997), 26.

5. Aubrey Daniels, *Bringing Out the Best in People: How to Apply the Astonishing Power of Positive Reinforcement* (New York: McGraw-Hill, 1999), 49.

6. Crabb, *Connecting,* 12.

7. Richard Carlson, *Don't Sweat the Small Stuff* (New York: Hyperion, 1997), 193.

8. Dr. Ron Jenson, *Make a Life, Not Just a Living* (Nashville: Broadman & Holman, 1995), 22.

Chapter 5

1. Stu Weber, *Tender Warrior: God's Intention for a Man* (Sisters, Ore.: Multnomah Publishing, 1999), 187.

2. Dr. Richard Halverson, in James Osterhaus, *Bonds of Iron: Forging Lasting Male Relationships* (Chicago: Moody Publishers, 1994), 92.

3. Ibid., 92.

4. Crabb, *Connecting,* 38.

5. Sears, 139.

Chapter 6

1. Gordon MacDonald, *Renewing Your Spiritual Passion* (Thomas Nelson, 1989), 171.

2. Gary Thomas, *Seeking the Face of God* (Nashville: Thomas Nelson, 1994), 102.

Chapter 7

1. Jenson, *Make a Life, Not Just a Living,* 53.

2. Dr. Howard Hendricks, professor at Dallas Theological Seminary and former chaplain for the Dallas Cowboys, in audiotape, *Accountability: Making an Impact by Being Authentic.*

Chapter 8

1. Jenson, *Make a Life, Not Just a Living,* 1995.

2. Benner, 71.

3. Daniel Goleman, *Primal Leadership: Realizing the Power of Emotional Intelligence,* in The Harvard Business Review, 2001.
4. Benner, 70.
5. Crabb, *Connecting,* 127.

Chapter 9

1. Henri Nouwen, *The Wounded Healer* (New York: Doubleday, 1972), 63.
2. Michael B. McCaskey, "The Hidden Messages Managers Send," *The Harvard Business Review,* 1979.
3. Crabb, *The Silence of Adam* (Grand Rapids, Mich.: Zondervan, 1995), 99.

Chapter 10

1. Within the Young President's Organization, a breach of confidentially is grounds for immediate expulsion from a forum.
2. Larry Crabb, *The Silence of Adam,* 164.

Chapter 11

1. Crabb, *The Silence of Adam,* 69.
2. Steve Arterburn and Fred Stoeker, with Mike Yorkey, *Every Man's Battle: Every Man's Guide to Winning the War on Sexual Temptation One Victory at a Time* (Colorado Springs, Colo.: WaterBrook Press, 2000), 4.
3. Dr. Howard Hendricks, professor at Dallas Theological Seminary and former chaplain for the Dallas Cowboys, in audiotape, *Accountability: Making an Impact by Being Authentic,* DTS Tape Ministry.
4. Crabb, *Connecting,* 82.
5. James Osterhaus, *Bonds of Iron: Forging Lasting Male Relationships* (Moody Press, 1994), 153.
6. Socrates, in Plato, *Analogy.*

Chapter 12

1. Dr. William Gairdner, *The War against the Family* (New York: Stoddart, 1992).
2. Benner, 70.

Chapter 13

1. Jerry Johnston, *How to Save Your Kids from Ruin* (Colorado Springs, Colo.: Chariot Victor Publishing, 1999).
2. Ibid., 44.
3. Zig Ziglar, *Raising Positive Kids in a Negative World* (New York: Ballantine Books, 1985), 293.
4. Ibid., 322.
5. Ibid., 52.

Chapter 14

1. Gilbert Meilander. *Friendship: A Study In Theological Ethics* (London: University of Notre Dame Press, 1981).
2. Lewis, *The Four Loves,* 80.
3. C. S. Lewis, *God in the Dock* (Grand Rapids, Mich.: Eerdmans, 1944), 55.

Chapter 15

1. Dr. K. Cooper, *Faith-Based Fitness* (Nashville: Thomas Nelson, 1977), 20.
2. Ibid., 19.

Chapter 16

1. Peter Legge, personal communication.
2. Jimmy Pattison with Paul Grescoe, *Jimmy: An Autobiography* (New York: McClelland-Bantam), 1987.

Chapter 17

1. MacDonald, *Renewing Your Spiritual Passion,* 69.
2. MacDonald, *Spiritual Passion,* 69.
3. Ibid., 171.
4. John Fisher, *A Guide to Prayer for All God's People* (Nashville: Upper Room Books, 1990).
5. C. S. Lewis, *The Letters of C. S.Lewis to Arthur Greeves* (New York: Collier Books, 1916), 104.

Part IV

1. C. S. Lewis, *The Four Loves,* Harcourt Brace and Company, 1960, 57.

Chapter 18

1. Based on Isaiah 9:6.
2. Gary Thomas, *Seeking the Face of God* (Nashville: Thomas Nelson, 1994), 113.
3. Benner, 77.

Chapter 19

1. Stu Weber, *Locking Arms* (Sisters, Ore.: Multnomah Publishers, 1995), 159.

Appendix

1. Dr. Mitch Whitman, personal communication.
2. Weber, *Locking Arms,* 191.
3. Ibid., 191.

Other Resources from Augsburg

Rediscovering Friendship by Elisabeth Moltmann-Wendel
136 pages, 0-8006-3445-4

In an honest and meditative style, Moltmann-Wendel finds in friendship new dimensions of adventure, consolation, self-knowledge, love, and political relevance, as well as profound resonances with Jesus's friendships with women, especially Mary Magdalene, and with his friends at the Last Supper.

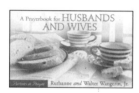

A Prayerbook for Husbands and Wives
by Ruthanne and Walter Wangerin Jr.
128 pages, 0-8066-4062-6

This unique collection aims to make prayer a powerful joint activity that will weave strong relationships between the readers themselves and between the readers and God.

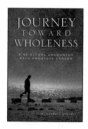

Journey toward Wholeness by R. Carroll Stegall
224 pages, 0-8066-4595-4

The story of Stegall's experience with prostate cancer. Stegall brings his gifts as a storyteller and his perspective as a person of faith to a work that informs and helps enable cancer-sufferers (especially men) and their families to better articulate their fears, anxieties, and hopes as they stuggle through the experience.

A Good Friend for Bad Times
by Deborah E. Bowen and Susan L. Strickler
144 pages, 0-8066-5151-2

Addresses how to support a family before and immediately after a death and in the weeks and years beyond. Also provides insight for situations involving Alzheimer's disease, cancer, AIDS, suicide, and the death of a child, among others.

Available wherever books are sold.